LAUGHTER
at the
FESTIVE BOARD

LAUGHTER at the FESTIVE BOARD

*ANECDOTES, JOKES, QUIPS AND WITTICISMS
FOR MASONIC AFTER DINNER SPEAKERS*

by **GEOFFREY BRYAN**

First published in England in 1996

© 1996 Geoffrey Bryan

The rights of Geoffrey Bryan to be identified as author of this work has been asserted by him in accordance with the Copyright, Design and Patents Act, 1988.

Published by Ian Allan Regalia Ltd
Coombelands House, Coombelands Lane
Addlestone, Surrey, KT15 1HY
who are members of the Ian Allan Group

ISBN 0 853182124

British Library Cataloguing in Publication.
A record for this book is available from the British Library.

All rights reserved. No part of this book may be reproduced or transmitted in any form or by any means, electronic or mechanical, including photocopying, recording or by any information storage and retrieval system, without permission of the Publisher in writing.

The cartoons included in this book are the copyright of the author.

Printed and bound in Great Britain
by Latimer Trend & Company Ltd, Plymouth

DEDICATION

I dedicate this slim volume to my wife Pauline and to my children, Donna and Matthew, who thought that all the time I was working on my computer with this book I was only playing computer games.

ABOUT THE AUTHOR

Geoffrey Bryan is the pseudonym of an Essex mason who joined the Craft in 1975. He is married and lives in Wickford with his wife and two cats. He has two children, both chefs, who live away from home.

Geoff worked as a Personnel Manager with the London office of a large Australian bank. He was with the bank for almost twenty seven years.

Apart from masonry, Geoff is interested in Calligraphy, Hand-made continental style chocolates (making them, not eating them), Personal Computers and in collecting more anecdotes, jokes for another volume of Masonic humour.

ACKNOWLEDGEMENTS

I have to acknowledge the help given to me by friends and acquaintances in the construction of the anecdotes, jokes, witticisms contained in this book. These stories, etc., have been told to me over some twenty or so years and I am unable in virtually all cases to give acknowledgements to any one person whether mason or non-mason.

I apologise in advance to the many, many people whom I cannot name but I confirm that they are much thought of, well regarded and their efforts are really appreciated.

Those friends I can actually remember as being suppliers of humourous stories and support over many years and to whom I extend my warmest thanks are Chris Crane, Roy Howard, Ken Todd and Don Tucker.

INTRODUCTION

Masonic anecdotes and jokes have been part of our Masonic culture for many, many years. Whilst, I am against jokes that set our craft up for ridicule I truly feel that Freemasonry is a vibrant organisation and can and should benefit from humour.

The many Masonic speeches and replies to toasts, which a mason hears in a Masonic lifetime are nearly always so much better appreciated when they include humour of some kind, especially when the humour is well told.

The anecdotes, jokes and witticisms enclosed in this small volume have been gathered at meetings, at Festive Boards and by brethren coming up to me and telling me their stories or jokes they have invented or heard from others. I regret that I cannot give acknowledgements to any specific brother for these contributions. Several versions of the same stories and jokes have been told to me by different people, they couldn't tell me where they had heard, or even read, them.

All I hope is that a brother will read and enjoy these stories and use them in his Masonic speech making. Let us hope that he gets his laughs and in so doing gets a Masonic point over which might not have happened without the joke.

I accept that there is a plethora of books on after dinner speaking, on anecdotes, and joke books. Many are on general subjects but there appear to be books for after dinner speakers on most subjects under the sun.

Unfortunately, there is a shortage of books on Masonic humour. The slim volumes that I have seen seem more to reflect American anecdotal humour. In my opinion this type of humour doesn't always travel to the United Kingdom too well. Where books appear in the specialist book shop purporting to be on Masonic humour they seem to contain a very limited number of Masonic jokes bulked out by non-Masonic humour.

If, you find the available books useful and you have the time to adapt their contents to Masonic situations then good luck to you. If, as I have found, the contents take too long to adapt and fit into your speech then I hope that this book will prove of use to you.

I have not put the jokes, limericks, anecdotes into a thematic format as fifteen jokes one after the other on, say, the Festive Board will become boring. I call this the lore of diminishing Masonic returns.

To all my brothers in the craft I greet you all well.

Geoffrey Bryan 1996

N.B. It has not been my intention to give away any private information that should properly only be imparted behind the closed door of the lodge room. If I have been in any way amiss then it is my fault alone and I hope that you will accept my apology in advance. Mia Culpa.

Laughter at the Festive Board

☐

THE CLEANEST APRON is the one worn by the newly made Master Mason.

☐

IRWIN AND RALPH were keen on anthropology and both graduated from university with first class degrees. They joined the same old boys lodge and both went through the chair. Ralph eventually got married but, after several years, was persuaded with Irwin to join an expedition sponsored by the university.

When they reached Africa they had an extremely hard time with the natives. They seemed to hate all white men with a vengeance. Undaunted the lodge brothers stayed together through all adversities.

One evening after a very trying day Irwin said:

"Ralph, I have a big confession to make. The only reason I am on this trip is to gather information for a large oil conglomerate who will be paying me about £1,000,000. You will only be getting a small amount from the University."

"Irwin, I have an even bigger confession to make. The real reason why I came on the trip was because my seven year old daughter has taken up violin lessons".

☐

A PRECEPTOR was taking his time
At the lodge of instruction divine
The angels were fit
In Aldersgate's wit
But their Taylors sure did lack the rhyme.

☐

GAUNTLETS: coverings for senior officers' cuffs that keep the soup out of the suit.

☐

THE BADGE of a mason shows that
He's a man who plays with a straight bat
He believes in the truth
Fraternity, youth
And money to put in the hat.

Laughter at the Festive Board

□

OLD LODGES never die they only loose their warrants.

□

KIDS AND MASONRY don't always go together. A mason's thirteen year old son saw him getting ready for lodge one Saturday. He saw him get out his black tie and white cotton gloves and asked if he was going out to sing like Al Jolson. His father laughed and shook his head. The boy continued to watch his father as he took his regalia case down from the top of the wardrobe. He asked if it contained a musical instrument like the one's used in the Salvation Army. His father again laughed and tried to convince him he had neither a clarinet nor a tuba in the case but he didn't look that convinced.

Finally, he needed to open his case and the boy saw the blue apron strapped inside.

"Dad, let me give you some advice. If you're going out to do the washing up the apron will be all right but shouldn't you use Marigold rubber gloves? Those white cotton gloves look nice now but once you've put them in water, your hands will get all wrinkly, a bit like your neck".

He smiled his special thank you to his son, -the washing up expert.

□

OVERHEARD IN a pub (I know it's a calumny but if we can't take it we shouldn't have gone through all the aggravation and joined).

A rich freemason, a poor freemason and Father Christmas were walking together along a road when they saw a £10 note in their path.

Who picked the note up?

The rich freemason, of course. The other two are figments of people's imagination.

□

A LITTLE BOY was watching his grandad getting ready to go off to lodge. He saw him get his regalia case out and put it on the bed. He watched as he put his nice white shirt on. But when he put his black tie on and then his Masonic cufflinks he said:

"Grandad, do you know that when you put your black tie on and put your shirt jewellery (cuff links?) on, you are always so poorly the next morning?"

☐

THREE MASONS were having a drink after the meeting and they got into the philosophic conversation of when life begins.

The first, a Mormon said: "At conception."

The second, a Baptist said: "At birth."

The third, a Jew, shook his head and smiling said: "Brothers, forgive me but you are both wrong. Life begins when the dog dies and the kids leave home."

☐

BERT AND RODNEY had been lodge brothers for twenty years. Their wives were also very friendly and the four of them decided to go on a Mediterranean cruise together. They joined a large liner at Southampton but their happiness at their State Suite was shattered on the first night.

Their steward knocked on their door and when they opened it he said:

"Excuse me, Sirs and Madams but the captain would be delighted if you would like to join him for dinner this evening at his table."

"Who do you navy people think we are?" said a very indignant Bert "We've paid a hell of a lot of money for this cruise and you tell us that we've got to dine with the crew."

☐

AFTER A MEETING a mason brought a lodge brother home for coffee. They both sat down and one requested his put upon wife, to get them both a coffee. She had been up to her armpits in washing the whole day and was near exhaustion. She couldn't be bothered to make fresh percolated coffee so she made them both instant.

The guest, looked at the colour of the liquid with a critical eye and smelt it. He gingerly tasted the black liquid and asked:

"Where was this coffee made, my dear?"

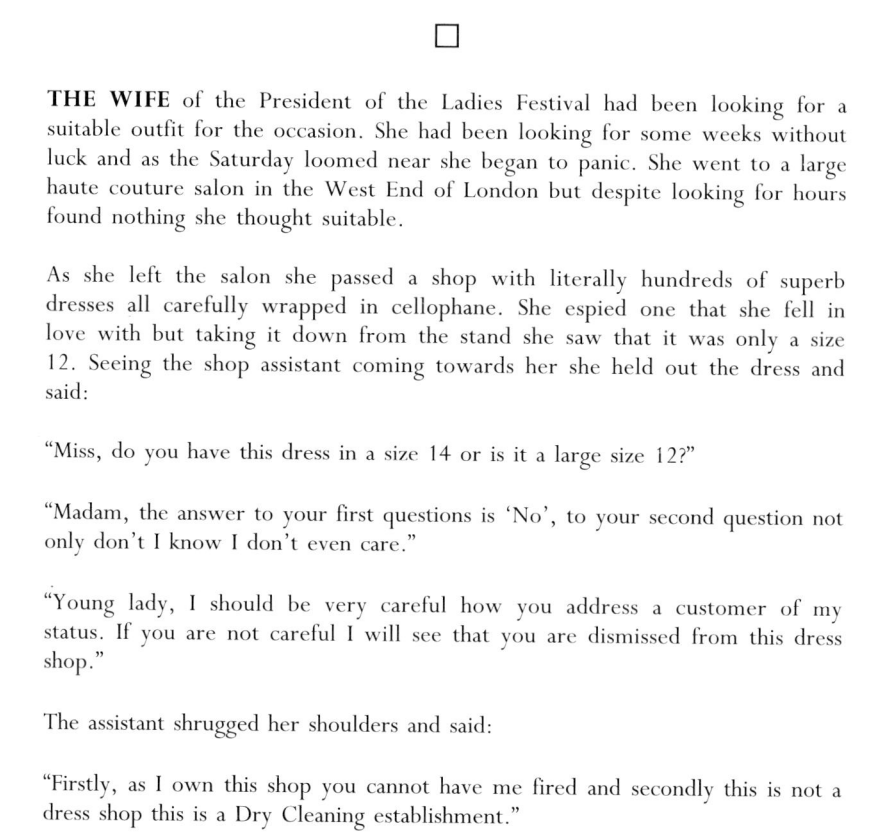

Laughter at the Festive Board

"Why, in the kitchen," she replied.

"Such a shame it doesn't travel well"

□

THE WIFE of the President of the Ladies Festival had been looking for a suitable outfit for the occasion. She had been looking for some weeks without luck and as the Saturday loomed near she began to panic. She went to a large haute couture salon in the West End of London but despite looking for hours found nothing she thought suitable.

As she left the salon she passed a shop with literally hundreds of superb dresses all carefully wrapped in cellophane. She espied one that she fell in love with but taking it down from the stand she saw that it was only a size 12. Seeing the shop assistant coming towards her she held out the dress and said:

"Miss, do you have this dress in a size 14 or is it a large size 12?"

"Madam, the answer to your first questions is 'No', to your second question not only don't I know I don't even care."

"Young lady, I should be very careful how you address a customer of my status. If you are not careful I will see that you are dismissed from this dress shop."

The assistant shrugged her shoulders and said:

"Firstly, as I own this shop you cannot have me fired and secondly this is not a dress shop this is a Dry Cleaning establishment."

□

AFTER A MEETING a distinguished Masonic visitor was retrieving his overcoat from the cloakroom. He was not given a cloakroom ticket when he deposited his coat and when the attendant gave him the coat he looked at it and said in a rather supercilious way:

"Young man, how do you know that this is my coat?"

"I don't sir, but that is the coat you handed to me when you came in."

Laughter at the Festive Board

☐

A FRENCH MASON came as a guest of an English mason to a lodge meeting. At the Festive Board a fly was buzzing around the table and the Englishman wishing to impress his French guest pointed his knife at the offending insect and said:

"Monsieur, regardez le moche."

"No, no, my friend. "La" moche. You see "the fly" is feminine."

"Francois, you really have got fabulous eyesight."

☐

A YOUNG MAN was being interviewed by the Master and lodge officers prior to him being balloted for the lodge.

The master, an old campaigner with a glass eye, was giving the young man a very hard time and seemed to override all the simple questions being put to him by his officers.

"Young man, I have noticed that for the last ten minutes you have been staring at me." said the master gruffly, "do you know that I have a glass eye? I bet that you don't know which one it is, do you?"

"Yes, sir. It is the right one," he replied without hesitation.

"That's remarkable. How could you tell that from where you are sitting?"

"It was easy. It's the friendly one."

☐

THE LADIES FESTIVAL was being held at a large London Hotel in the "Royalty Room". The master and his lady got out of their taxi and asked the door man the way to the "Garden Room".

"Oh yes sir, go straight along the hall and turn left and you will find "The Palms" directly in front of you."

"I'm sorry we want the "Royalty Room" not "The Palms" corrected the master.

"Please forgive me sir. They are the same room. When you see the waiters there with their hands held out you will realise why the staff always refer to it as "The Palms".

□

THE WIFE OF THE IPM was arranging the Ladies' Festival with the new hotel manageress. There was a lot to get through and the hotel manageress was looking decidedly uncertain with all the details that had to be right for the occasion.

"Please excuse my uncertainty but this will be my first large-scale ladies' night and I might well forget some insignificant little detail"

"My dear, you mustn't worry. I'll see that the master gets here."

□

THE WIFE OF THE LODGE master looked at her husband in bed and said:

"Basil, this morning I saw Joan, the wife of your lodge secretary and she said that your lodge was all wine, women and song."

"Like all wives she's got it wrong. I can categorically confirm that there is very little to sing about in our lodge."

□

IT WAS coming up for the master's twenty-fifth wedding anniversary and his wife tackled him.

"Have you forgotten that it's our silver wedding day in a month's time. How shall we celebrate it?"

Without hesitation the master replied:

"I think that two minute's silence would be appropriate."

□

BEHIND EVERY SUCCESSFUL MASON is a dedicated wife and an incredulous mother in law.

□

THE CANDIDATE on his application form to join the lodge put his employment as "Visual display technician" but changed it to "Window Cleaner" when the Treasurer asked him how to correct a problem on his personal computer.

A SILLY MM from Cawnpore
Had a habit that lodges abhor
He would loosen his belt
Of his apron and felt
Happy as it fell to the floor.

☐

THE IPM was in some distress sitting to the right of the Worshipful Master. He was fidgeting in his chair and several Grand Lodge Officers near him were tut-tutting as he squirmed. The master leaned over to him and using his gauntlet to shield his mouth asked what was his problem.

"Sorry, master, but I have had a bit of a tiff with the wife this morning and in revenge she has double starched my underpants."

☐

MANY TIMES have you heard it said
That masons are always well bred
But here and there
Please have a care
'Cause cowans are easily led.

☐

OLD LODGES never die they just get renumbered.

☐

TWO SIBLINGS who had never really got on were both attending a lodge as guests of two members. As they met at the Festive Board they nodded to one another but it was obvious that something was going to be said.

As the waitress brought the first course one brother, who was extremely thin, declined the fried white bait and requested a small portion of melon.

"Gerald, what is the matter with you, man?" said his very portly brother "you look like you've just come from a famine area."

"From the look of you, Robert, you look like the person who caused it."

☐

IF MASONS cannot always be called pillars of society that can at least be there to help knock the sharp edges off these pillars.

☐

MASONIC VISITORS are known to be ritually critical.

☐

DURING THE LAST WAR a lodge in London had trouble with their organ. The master had spoken to the lodge organist about having more control of his instrument but he could do little as he could not get the parts necessary to put it back into good working order. On one particular occasion after the lodge resumed after the "all clear" had gone the brethren resumed but within five minutes the organ began it's high pitched wail. The master stood up and said to the organist:

"Brother John, either your organ is having intestinal difficulties or the siren has failed to warn of the return of a lone Dornier."

☐

AN INITIATE returned home to his mother who gave him a bit of a grilling as to what had happened during his initiation.

─────────────── **Laughter at the Festive Board** ───────────────

"Mum, as much as I would like to tell you what happened I cannot. I have agreed not to tell anyone what happens in lodge."

"Look, John, I am your mother. I am sure that when they asked you not to tell anyone they didn't mean that you were to keep it from me-your own mother."

"I'm sorry, mum, but even if I wanted to, I couldn't tell you much because for a lot of the time I didn't see what was happening."

"Very well, John. But next time I want you to sit nearer the front."

☐

THE LATECOMER to the meeting had difficulty finding a seat whilst a "third" was being conducted. Eventually he found a large seat which already had an occupant who was forced to move over. After a minute a voice whispered into his ear:

"I'm sorry to disturb you brother, but either you budge up a bit or you'll have to play this ruddy organ yourself in about ten seconds when the ritual finishes."

☐

A MAN went into a small restaurant and as he was being shown to a table he noticed a large sign on a wall. The sign read:

> *"NO FREEMASONS SERVED IN THIS ESTABLISHMENT-*
> *BY ORDER OF THE OWNER"*

"Excuse me, what has the owner against freemasons. As I am a freemason I would like to speak to him."

The waitress brought the owner of the establishment to the man's table and he said:

"I am sorry sir, but as you have admitted to my waitress that you are a freemason and as such I must insist that you leave."

"This really is ridiculous. But just a moment you are wearing a Masonic ring. Why, if you are in the craft, you stop other freemasons from eating here?"

The owner leaned over to him and whispered in his ear:

"Have you tasted the food?"

Laughter at the Festive Board

☐

THE NEWLY WEDS were in bed together when the wife said:

"Darling, you know that before we got married we promised never to have secrets from each other?"

"That's right, Bunnikins. No secrets we agreed."

"Well, darling, you are a freemason and have lots and lots of secrets and I think that you should tell me them."

"Bunnikins, it is very difficult but would you promise that you would keep any secrets told to you and never, never tell anyone else in the big wide world?"

"Darling, of course. If I was told a secret I wouldn't tell anyone - ever."

"That's good Bunnikins- neither would I." He kissed her on the forehead and turned over and went to sleep.

☐

A MASON returned home late one evening after a particularly pleasant Festive Board. He paid the taxi off and quietly opened the front door and tip toed up the stairs. As he entered the dark bedroom his wife woke up with a start.

"Bernard, is that you?"

"Why, who else were you expecting?"

☐

THE LODGE SECRETARY organised a trip for the lodge members to Paris. They went around by executive tourist coach to see all the city's important sights. As they were going through one district the tour guide said over the coach's speaker system:

"Brethren, on the right we are now passing the city's most infamous bordello."

"Why?" chorused three voices at the back of the coach.

―――――――― Laughter at the Festive Board ――――――――

☐

BILL AND DAPHNE were hosting a small dinner party with Bill's lodge brother Mark and his wife Carol. Bill's daughter Jenny, who was nine, wanted to stay up but Daphne told her that it was a grown up's party. Daphne reminded her of her promise to go to bed at eight o'clock before they all sat down to eat.

Jenny sulked, threw tantrums and much to Mark and Carol's annoyance Bill agreed for her to say "Grace" before the dinner and then to go straight up to bed.

When the dinner was laid out on the table and the four adults were seated Jenny came over to where her mother was seated. She whispered loudly into her mother's ear:

"Mummy, what have I got to say? I've forgotten."

"You silly old silly," smiled Daphne "just say what Daddy said at breakfast this morning."

Jenny closed her eyes and said:

"Daphne, we're not having those terrible people around for dinner again, are we?"

☐

A HUMOROUS MASTER of note
Was telling a joke on a boat
An ark mariner there
Threw him over with care
Just to see if the funny ones float

☐

TWO MASONS went on holiday to the Holy Land to look at the remains of Herod the Great's Temple at Jerusalem. They also took bus trips to Tel Aviv and to the old town of Tiberius on the Sea of Galilee. They looked at the magnificent blue waters and decided to have a boat trip to the other side of the inland lake. When they asked the boat owner how much for the excursion he demanded an exorbitant sum. When he saw the look of horror on their faces the Israeli smiled and said:

"Gentlemen, remember that this is the Lake Tiberius of your Bible. The place where Jesus of Nazareth walked on the water."

"At these prices," voiced one of them, "no wonder he walked."

☐

AN OLD WORSHIPFUL MASTER named Ben
Forgot his words again and again
Not now and again
But again and again
and again and again and again.

☐

AN INNER GUARD with nothing to do
Spent the meeting in cutting his shoe
With a poniard so sharp
At the end he would carp
'Cause his shoe fell to pieces - it's true.

☐

THE CANDIDATE stood there, white and meek
When the Master looked up and did speak
"Are you of age and free?"
He looked up with much glee
"It's my legs not my heart that are weak."

☐

THE YOUNG MAN stood hoodwinked, with tow,
Whilst the Tyler was by him to go
The many knocks were so loud
That the candidate cowered
But the Tyler was there toe to toe.

☐

WHAT HAPPENED when a dirty chip paper blew into a lodge and landed at the secretary's table? The master was prompted by the secretary to sign it.

Laughter at the Festive Board

□

A MAGISTRATE who was a mason was somewhat disturbed by the defendant in the dock, who was accused of dangerous driving, and kept making various Masonic signs of distress.

The magistrate stopped the defendant's unseemly behaviour by asking him why the defendant should not lose his driving licence for one year for driving on the pavement.

"Your honour, my livelihood depends on my driving," squirmed the mason.

"As does that of the pedestrians," retorted the magistrate.

□

AT A LARGE MEETING a senior Grand Lodge Officer was giving a lecture on The Early Lodges of the Eighteenth Century. As he began the second hour of his lecture the distinct sound of snoring shook the room. The lecturer stopped and looking up from his notes said in a stetorious voice:

"Would someone please wake up the brother who is snoring."

A voice from the back of the room shouted back:

"Look mate, you put him to sleep, you wake him up"

Laughter at the Festive Board

☐

THE SENIOR STEWARD took the joining brother, who was to be the new lodge steward, around the lodge room.

"Jeremy, as junior steward, part of your duties will be to see senior lodge members to their seats. Our senior masons are the nicest old chaps in masonry. The only thing I would say is that you ensure that no one is sitting in their seats when you bring the old chaps in. If someone is inadvertently sitting in their pew you will be witness to words only heard in the ladies cloakroom at Ladies Festivals."

☐

THE NEW MASTER was determined to please
By putting the initiate at ease
But knocking was heard
It was too absurd
"Sorry said the man "It's my knees"

☐

THE DIFFERENCE between a difficulty and an embarrassment is that a difficulty is when the master forgets his words. An embarrassment is when the initiate prompts him.

☐

A MASON went to pick up a friend to go with him to a meeting. As the friend was not quite ready he was asked to come into the house to wait for him.

The children were turning the house upside down, shouting, fighting and crying.

The wife came in and said to him philosophically:

"Sometimes, you know, I wish that I'd just loved and lost."

☐

AT THE LADIES FESTIVAL the elderly mason was talking to a lady to his right. Seeing that he was rather frail she asked him if he would like her to cut his meat up for him. He smiled and said:

"No thank you, dear lady. I'm quite used to meat this tough at my old people's home."

Laughter at the Festive Board

□

AFTER AN LOI one mason was bragging to his various cronies that he had no vices.

"Don't you drink alcohol at all?" asked one.

"Not a drop."

"Don't you smoke?" asked another.

"I smoke a small cigar after I have had a good meal. My darling wife's cooking has got me down to one cigar a month."

□

A MAN was talking to a friend and he said:

"I've decided to have a house built and I've employed an architect who is also a freemason to draw up the plans. I've just received his invoice for his fee and if he is a freemason I hesitate to think how much a dear mason would have charged."

□

A YOUNG MASON told the master that he was thinking of getting married.

The master looked at him and said:

"Ronnie, you must let me give you some sage advice. It is true that a man has more sense after he is married - unfortunately, by that time it is much too late."

□

A MASON was sitting on his door step at midnight when a policeman shone his light on him and asked him what he was doing at that hour.

"Officer, I have been to a lodge meeting and I have stupidly mislaid my key. I am just waiting for my sixteen year old daughter to arrive home so that she can let me in."

□

THE FAVOURITE PET of the mason was his dog but they both were in disgrace. The dog for wetting the family carpet, the mason for attending lodge on his wife's birthday. That it was his installation did not matter to his wife. He was sent out into the cold with his trusty dog.

After an hour he decided to have a drink and went into the nearest pub. However, he only just went through the door when he saw a large notice which said:

UNDER NEW MANAGEMENT - NO DOGS ALLOWED.

He looked at the dog and shrugged his shoulders and started to walk out. Just then a customer came out of the pub and asked him what was wrong. He pointed to the notice. The man sneered and said:

"It's only the new manager. He's not in tonight. Go and have a drink. If you are asked to leave, tell them that is a guide dog. They've got to let you in with a guide dog."

Thanking him the man and dog went in. As he reached the bar the new manager arrived and said:

"Can't you read the notice? Dogs are not allowed in this pub"

"Oh," said the man, "it's all right. The dog is a guide dog."

"Guide dog. Everyone's got guide dogs tonight. Look mate, let me tell you something; guide dogs are either Labrador's or German Shepherds."

Looking suitably blank at the wall above the manager's head the dog owner asked:

"Oh, what have they given me then?"

□

A VERY LARGE senior mason received Grand Lodge honours and as his father had received the same honours fifty years before he decided to wear his father's collar and apron. However, being a much larger man than his father both collar and apron were tight on him. He went to a large regalia shop near to where he lived and asked them if they could alter them to fit him.

"I'm sorry sir, but the age of these pieces of regalia is extremely old and the quality is poor. We would suggest that it would be much safer for you to shrink to fit them rather than they take the strain of stretching to fit you."

□

DURING WORLD WAR II a regimental lodge had it's colonel for it's master for the duration. The master was a stickler for protocol and was detested by all the lodge members from the major down to the privates.

In 1943 a sergeant and a private who were members of the lodge were on charges accused of kicking the colonel.

At their court martial the sergeant told his story that he had been doing his physical training exercises and was wearing his plimsolls. The colonel had come around the corner and had trodden on the sergeant's toes. The sergeant happened to have a bad corn and had kicked out before he realised who it was who had injured him.

The private said that there were mitigating circumstances in his case too. He had seen the sergeant kick the colonel and was sure that the war must be over and so he kicked the colonel as well.

□

A RICH MASON was called up for army service during the second world war. He was doing quite well but during his first week in the army he felt unwell and went on sick parade.

The army doctor was less than pleased at the numbers reporting unwell and he went up to the mason and said:

"Soldier, would you have wasted my time in Civvy Street and come to see me for this minor complaint you say you have?"

"No, sir, certainly not sir. In Civvy Street I would have sent for you."

□

BILL HAD attended lodge and as he came out it was raining cats and dogs. When he tried to put up his umbrella some spines were broken. When he got home he told his wife that he would take his damaged umbrella to the repairers. His wife asked him if he would also take two of her broken umbrellas.

On Monday he took the three umbrellas to the repairers and was asked to return on Tuesday when they would be ready for collection.

Laughter at the Festive Board

When he was on his train home he absentmindedly picked up an umbrella from the rack above his head. The man next to him told him that he was taking his umbrella. He apologised profusely and red-faced got off the train.

Next day, he collected the umbrellas and placed them, with their handles sticking out of the parcel, on the rack above him on the train. As his train arrived at his station he stood up and took the parcel off the rack. The man next to him smiled and said:

"Had a good day I see."

☐

A MASON was brought into the local police station by a beat officer. The desk sergeant asked him what he was being charged with.

"Drunkenness. He was on his hands and knees at a Zebra Crossing."

"That in itself doesn't mean that he was drunk does it officer?"

"No, but as he was trying to roll up the crossing saying that the lodge carpet was in need of cleaning does suggest that he was."

☐

A MASON who had just left the Festive Board slightly the worse for wear hailed a taxi.

He got in and sat down and said to the driver:

"My man, take me to the Roebuck Hotel."

"But this is the Roebuck Hotel mister!" replied the taxi driver scratching his head.

"Thank you. But next time don't drive so damned fast."

☐

A VISITOR criticising the lodge
Saw the workings were a bit of a bodge.
The Master used "Taylor's"
The Inner Guard - "Naylor's"
And the Past Master - a version of "Hodge."

AN OLD MASON died and his grandson was given the task of going through his regalia and other Masonic effects. The old gentleman had not attended lodge for many years and his gloves and apron were thick with dust. As he looked inside the pocket of the apron he found a yellowed shoe ticket for a pair of shoes taken for repairs twenty years before. He decided to see if the shoes were still in the shop and went there next day.

He presented the ticket and the aproned cobbler went into the back. He returned without the shoes and said:

"Yes, we have the shoes. They'll be ready for collection next Tuesday."

☐

OLD ASSISTANT SECRETARIES never die they just take hours with the minutes.

☐

A MASON was looking dejectedly into his gin and tonic at the hotel bar when a lodge brother came up to him and said:

"Hello, Bill. That was a good meeting this evening. Why are you looking so sad?"

"John, do you know how to stop a woman from being a nymphomaniac?"

"No," replied John with a quizzical look

"You marry her."

☐

A VISITING MASON was a theatrical talent scout and while sitting in lodge the Inner Guard did a magnificent front leap with a half twist.

Turning to his neighbour he said:

"That boy's tremendous. I could get him two weeks at the London Palladium doing that act."

"You'll have to book the Junior Warden as well. He's the one who just caught the Inner Guard's hand with his gavel."

☐

THE BRETHREN came to the Festive Board and when the master had been clapped in, sat down. Brother Fred Smith was hungry and by the time the lodge chaplain stood to say the Grace had already devoured four bread rolls and a bowl of soup.

"For what the lodge and it's guests are about to receive, and for what Brother Fred has already received, may the Lord make us truly thankful and ever mindful of the wants of other, S.M.I.B."

☐

THE MASTER AND HIS WIFE came to the hotel where the quarterly lodge meeting was being held. They signed in and the wife went up to their room.

"It must cost you a fortune, master, to stay overnight in this hotel." declared the IPM.

"Well, yes it does but I think it money well spent. I bring the wife here because it saves me having to kiss her goodbye."

☐

OLD MASONS never die they just keep chipping away.

☐

THE LODGE SECRETARY was at an installation meeting when he developed an extremely sore throat. The throat seemed to get worse and worse during the meeting and he had to get the outgoing IPM to read the minutes and the various communications out to the lodge. At the end of the meeting he excused himself to the new master and went straight to his private doctor.

The secretary, who was some 22 stone in weight, was certain that his doctor was going to lecture him again about his weight. He was pleasantly surprised that his doctor just examined his throat with a large wooden lolly stick and made a few notes on a pad.

"Mr Brown, please go behind that curtain and remove all your clothes."

He was somewhat surprised as he only had a sore throat but did as he was bid.

"Right. Now please would you go over to that corner and get onto your hands and knees."

This he did and the doctor went over to him and looked at him from all directions.

"Good, now go to the opposite side of the room and get on all fours again."

Again he complied and the doctor looked as before.

"That's excellent. Now please just go on all fours in front of me there."

"Excuse me doctor," he said hoarsely, "but can you tell me what's wrong with me?"

"Oh," said the doctor, "you've got a bad case of laryngitis. I'll give you a course of penicillin for it."

"Why did you get me to bend down in different parts of the room if I've only got laryngitis?"

"Well, I've got a white leather three piece suite coming tomorrow and I just wanted to see what it looked like in this room."

☐

A FARMER who was the current master of his lodge was in the dairy when his twelve year old son came in. The farmer was pouring the contents of one churn into another.

"Dad, are you pouring water into the milk churn?"

"No, son, I am pouring milk into this churn which is half full of water. When you are asked by anyone if I add water to the milk you can truthfully tell them that I do not. This illustrates an important principle that I have always advocated in lodge as in life. That it is better to cheat than to tell lies."

☐

DURING THE WAR a doctor was on the Medical Examination Board to pass or reject conscripts for active service in the army. Whilst he was at lodge one Saturday the master asked him how he was doing.

"Well," said the doctor, "it is very difficult at times to check out people who deliberately feign illness or some debility to stop getting called up."

"Last week, I examined a young man who said that he was nearly blind. All the tests showed that his eyes were perfect, no damage to the retinas, no glaucoma but at the end of the day he said he couldn't see more than a few feet from him and that was blurred. Eye glasses didn't help and so I had to agree that he was not fit to join up. I did tell him that he could be recalled at any time for re- examination."

"That was the end of that then?" remarked the master.

"Not quite. Yesterday. I went to the West End of London and went to the cinema. Where I unexpectedly sat next to the same young man. He didn't notice me and was thoroughly enjoying the film. I tapped him on the shoulder and he turned and recognised me immediately. But quick as a flash his eyes went into stares and he asked if the bus we were on went to Piccadilly."

☐

THE VICAR was a past master of his lodge and so was promoted to lodge chaplain. Doing all the things religious like saying the various lodge prayers and the grace at the Festive Board and ladies festivals. He also had the unpleasant task with the master of attending the funerals of brethren who had died.

One member of the lodge who died was a particularly obnoxious character and had been in prison on a number of occasions for various forms of villainy.

The wife of the deceased asked him, as someone who knew him well, if he would preside over his funeral. He discussed this with the master but neither could find anything nice to say about him. However, it was agreed that he should try even though it would be a very short eulogy at the graveside.

On the day of the funeral the lodge members and some of the deceased's family gathered around the grave side. They all looked to the vicar who said:

"We all knew brother Gordon either as head of his family or as a lodge brother. Many here will not know that he had an elder brother called Francis-well Francis was worse than Gordon." End of eulogy.

☐

THE FESTIVE BOARD was over and several of the hard drinkers retired to the hotel bar for their "night caps". After about six double gins one of their number stood up and staggered towards the door when he lost his footing and collapsed in a heap.

"That's what I like about our master," said one, "he always knows when to stop."

A GOOD MEMORY has always been a great asset to members of the craft. The various ritual books are not allowed in most lodges and so our rituals have to be learnt off by heart. In the early days the rituals themselves were not allowed to be written down in any way and learning by rote was the normal method of remembering.

Many lodges have brethren who are from the world of entertainment. Actors, comedians and others whose very livelihood depends on their good memories. These individuals are looked up to by the many brethren whose minds go completely blank when they have to stand up in open lodge to present the working tools or even when they are passed or raised.

One brother who had difficulty with learning his words had wanted to become master of his lodge more than anything. He needed key words written down to be able to go through the three degrees. He used to write the key words down at home and put the scrap of paper in front of him on his podium hidden from prying eyes by his gauntlet.

During one meeting he glanced at the paper and read to himself:

"2 pounds Onions, 1 pound Carrots, 3 Oranges...., Oh my God, Sainsbury's checkout has got my ritual notes."

THE MASTER was talking to the lodge secretary and said:

"Look Jack, I've notice that in lodge many of the brethren are rather short with me and some of them ignore me completely. Tell me the truth, what have I done to deserve such treatment?"

"Well, master, they are only human beings and your attitude to them is overbearing, rude and derogatory when you talk to them."

The master pondered for a moment then said:

"I agree that I have acted in that way, but it is only on those occasions when they dare to disagree with me."

☐

TWO MASON'S wives were talking about their respective husbands.

"My husband is infuriating. He will talk in his sleep."

"You're lucky. My husband doesn't talk at all; he just lies there asleep with a stupid grin on his face and every now and again he chuckles."

☐

CANDIDATES are lead to do it.

☐

A FARMER AND A VICAR attended the same lodge and after a meeting were discussing the merits of the craft.

"Freemasonry is like a farm on which small seeds of wisdom are sowed and by careful nurturing the seeds grow into sturdy plants which themselves bring forth seeds."

"I think rather that freemasonry is more like heaven where all one's wants are provided and the company is cheerful."

A brother passing overheard them said:

"You both have the wrong ideas of freemasonry. Freemasonry is a philosophical discipline in which the good learn and teach others. The bad don't learn and moan about the conditions of the lodge room and then they drift away."

□

A FORMER MASON who had left the craft under a cloud was going to give a lecture at the London Connaught Rooms on what was wrong with the UK Grand Lodge and the current Grand Lodge Officers.

On the day of the lecture a man went into a supermarket in Drury Lane and asked to speak to the manager.

"I would like to buy up all your old vegetables and all your bad and broken eggs that you have been unable to sell. I am going to the Connaught Rooms tonight."

"Oh, I see," said the manager "and you want to throw them at the lecturer for what he's going to say about the Grand Lodge people."

"Certainly not. I am the lecturer and I want the vegetables and bad eggs near me for self defence."

□

THE LODGE SECRETARY was looking blankly into his gin and tonic at the hotel bar when he was joined by the master. He bought the master a large whisky and soda and the master said:

"Well, Bill how's it going. Good attendance today I thought."

"Yes, master. I am extremely optimistic about the future of the lodge."

"But you are looking so down in the mouth. What's the matter old chap?"

"To be honest I'm not a hundred per cent sure that my optimism is really justified."

□

WHAT HAVE a naval destroyer and a lodge treasurer in common? They both are sub-chasers.

□

THE NEWLY MADE mason was sitting for the first time (and for many years the last time) at the top table sitting next to the Master. He was much enjoying himself when a junior steward with shaking hands managed to splash the brother initiate with wine.

The steward was full of apologies and began to dab the very wet brother with his handkerchief. The master saw his unhappiness and said to him:

"Brother steward, I think that you must have come to us from the Baptists but in freemasonry we initiate our new brother we do not baptise him."

□

A YOUNG MASON came into the lodge with a large black eye. His friends gathered around him to find where he got of his 'shiner'.

"If you nosy lot want to know I got it from my girl friend's husband."

"Serves you right you young rip," said a brother, "but, I thought he was away up North for the weekend."

"So did I," the black eyed brother replied ruefully, "So did I."

□

BRETHREN who like a small tipple will know, and I am sure give a wide berth, to so called "Dry Lodges", i.e. Lodges which do not allow intoxicating drinks at their premises.

A visitor at one such lodge had sat through a long "third" and a "second" with a full lecture on the Tracing Board. Before the Festive Board was set up he left the lodge rooms and in desperation walked up to the nearest gentleman and asked:

"Would you direct me to the nearest boozer, old man?"

"Mister," smiled the man, "you are looking at him."

□

TWO MASONS were at the bar and one said:

"Terrible about the Master being sent to that health clinic to dry out."

"I've heard that he is undergoing extreme torture there," replied the other, "all they are allowing him to live on seven days a week is food and water."

BILL had a terrible memory. When we went before the panel of freemasons prior to entering the craft he was told what would be expected of him. He was told the need for regular attendance at both LOI and quarterly lodge meetings. They also told him that he would have to learn and be able to remember the rituals without reference to any book Bill assured the lodge officers that he would do his very best and he joined the lodge.

Bill was determined to be a good mason and in order to train his memory he bought several memory improvement books.

He studied his ritual book at every spare moment and with his memory aids became word perfect in the rituals. The preceptor and master of ceremonies were really happy with his Masonic education and everyone in the lodge looked to him to really be a terrific master when his year of office came.

After a particularly taxing time at the office Bill decided to take his mobile phone "off the hook" and settle down to a relaxing game of golf with a non-Masonic friend.

After they had finished their game they went to the club house for a refreshing drink and Bill said:

"Bert, I really like my Masonry. It's a shame that you are not in the craft because I would have very much have liked you to come as my guest next Saturday. I am going into the chair as master of my lodge next Saturday, the 14th around 4 o'clock."

His friend looked at him very oddly.

"You mean the 21st, don't you, old boy? It's already 6 o'clock on the 14th now."

☐

THE LODGE TREASURER was looking very concerned and said to his assistant:

"Derek, I've just gone through the petty cash box and have found £50 missing. Now, only two people have got the keys - you and me."

"Well, why don't we both put in £25 and say no more about it?"

☐

A MASTER with a great deal to do
Spent most of his time in the loo
He sat hard on the seat
Ritual book at his feet
But nervous tummy made him feel blue.

☐

THE LODGE TREASURER was at home going through the lodge accounts when the phone rang.

"Mr Johnson, my name is Simpson, I am the manager of the Westlands Bank where your lodge has it's current account. As a signatory to that account I must inform you had the account is overdrawn some £1,325.56. What arrangements will you be making to put the account into order?"

"Mr Simpson, do you happen to have the statements of the lodge's account for the past year. If so what was the balance on the account as at close of business on 31 March?"

"Why it was £625 in credit."

"Did I phone you up?" the treasurer with a large smile on his face replaced the receiver.

☐

HARRY SMITH woke up with a fuzzy head but that didn't seem to be the reason for the frosty reception he got from his wife at breakfast.

"Why are you so sullen, my darling? When I came home from the lodge meeting last night I didn't make any noise at all."

"Perhaps you didn't make a noise but the four men, who were carrying you, most certainly did."

☐

A STEWARD by the name of Bill Todd
Ran right out of white wine, silly sod,
A past master with gout
Wanted Bill Todd chucked out
But the lodge got him back on the nod.

THE TWO BROTHERS at the Ladies Festival were standing at the bar.

"What can I get you?" asked one.

"I'd love something long very cold and full of gin" replied the other

"You must come over and meet my wife."

☐

A SINISTER BROTHER named Bert
Came into the lodge with no shirt
He threatened a brother
Made fun of another
He'll be asked to resign - that's a cert.

☐

TWO MASONS were at the bar after a meeting.

"Let me buy you a large whisky, Bill. After that meeting I think we all deserve a large drink."

"Gerald, you know that I have been a lifelong teetotaller. I only drink orange juice or mineral water. Do you know how many people die of liver damage caused by drinking?"

"I think that you have got to keep things in perspective," said Gerald, "Take my grandad for example. He drank a bottle of whisky or vodka every day of his adult life. He died when he was ninety four and the undertaker had to beat his liver to death with the coffin lid."

☐

THE GRAND LODGE OFFICER was giving the lodge a lecture on King Solomon's Temple in the light of modem finds in Archaeology. The brethren had to be coerced into 'putting on a good turnout' for the great man and many had come already liquidly refreshed in anticipation of a boring lecture.

The lecturer was introduced by the master but the noise only momentarily went down. As the lecturer was about to begin three or four groups of brethren began to laugh and shout to each other across the room. The lecturer took off his glasses and addressed the lodge:

"Brethren, I have no intention of beginning my most interesting lecture until the room has completely settled down."

A lone voice from the side said:

"Quite right, mate. Why don't you go home and sleep it off?"

☐

A NEWLY MADE MASON when raised
Told the lodge they would be amazed
At the speed he would learn
Not a head he did turn
But imagine the eyes overglazed

☐

THE CANDIDATE looked quiet and forlorn
As the light of a new way was born
He stood up, straight and tall
And was cheered by them all
But inside him he felt such a prawn.

☐

A RED NOSED BROTHER with a very bad disposition went to the hotel bar. The barman asked him if he would like a beer or a lager.

"Do you think that I look like someone who would drink beer or lager?"

"I'm sorry, sir. How do you like your Sarson's in a long or a short glass?"

☐

TWO MASONS met at their local bar. One was bruised around the forehead and mouth.

"You don't look to well, Fred. Did you fall over on the way home from the meeting last night?"

"No, I didn't fall over. My darling wife was waiting for me behind the kitchen door with a rolling pin. But it doesn't matter, I was going to have my front teeth taken out soon anyway."

☐

A DRUNK came off the street to the where the lodge was half way through the Festive Board when the toasts were being offered.

He grabbed a glass of wine from a steward and shouted at the top table:

"Let's all wish the bride and groom every happiness for the coming years."

"Hush, sir," said the nearest brother, "this is a Masonic meeting, you must leave at once."

"Whatever, it is" replied the drunk, "it sure is a hell of a party."

TWO MASONS had had a verbal exchange in the lodge and the master asked them to settle their difficulties outside. This they did but the raised voices turned into a full fledged fight outside. Damage to one of the brother's face was caused and the police decided to prosecute the offender.

The Tyler had witnessed the affray and was called as a witness for the prosecution.

"Did you see my client actually bite off the ear off Mr Smith?" asked defending counsel.

"No, sir, I did not," replied the Tyler.

"Then how do you know that he committed the offence."

"I saw the accused spit the ear out."

☐

THE HOTEL RECEPTIONIST took a telephone call.

"Could I speak to someone who is at the Ladies Festival being held in your ball room this evening? His name is Mr Hazelberg von Neufchatel auf Nordendorf."

"Certainly I will have Mr Hazelberg von Neufchatel auf Nordendorf paged. Please may I have his initials?"

☐

A SCOTTISH BROTHER woke up to find that his wife had passed over peacefully in her sleep.

He rang the bell for the maid and as she came in he said to her:

"Doreen, only one egg and soldiers for breakfast, this morning."

☐

THE MASTER AND HIS LADY WIFE were being driven to the Ladies Festival when their car was involved in a collision. Only the master was injured, both the wife and their driver, accompanied the master to the hospital in an ambulance.

The wife was with the master when the consultant came in and after listening to the injured man's chest covered his face with the sheet.

"I'm afraid that your husband is dead," he said solemnly.

"No, I'm not." said a voice from under the sheet.

"Gerald," snapped his wife, "don't argue with the consultant."

☐

THE MASTER was concerned at the health of his elderly mother and called a doctor, who was a brother at his lodge. The doctor did a thorough check up of the frail old lady and left a bottle of linctus for her to take.

As the master let the doctor out his mother called for him.

"I haven't seen that young man before who was he?" she asked.

"Oh, that was the doctor," replied her son.

"Yes, I thought that he was a little familiar for the vicar."

☐

INITIATES do it under guidance.

☐

THE PROFESSOR at the university college hospital asked a student doctor what he would do if a patient was brought to him who had swallowed a coin.

"Why, I would get my father to contact his lodge's treasurer. My father says that he could get money out of anyone."

☐

A MAGISTRATE was in his lodge discussing a recent case with the master.

"Children today are sorely in need of adult care and supervision. Yesterday, for instance, a boy of thirteen came up before me accused of stealing sweets from a small corner shop."

"Young man," I said "if you go on like this you will soon be up before me for robbing banks."

"I don't think that's very likely," he replied, "they don't let me out of school until 3.45."

☐

A MASON was at the hotel bar laughing one minute and howling the next. The lodge secretary passed him then turned and asked him what was the trouble.

"I had some very good news and some extremely bad news. I've just learned that my mother in law has gone over the cliff at Beachy Head in my brand new Volvo."

Laughter at the Festive Board

☐

AN INNER GUARD with poignard so sharp
Cut his finger and was heard to carp
"This weapons not fair
As it sliced through the air
When you play it like a small Irish harp."

☐

PAST MASTER who now holds Grand Rank
Walks round lodge like an old crank
It's not that he creaks
Through the whole of the weeks
But by wearing two collars that clank.

☐

OUR OLD TYLER who loved vindaloo
Had to make a quick dash for the loo
The knocks on the door
Had a waiter in awe
The Inner Guard shouted "Where's Hugh?"

☐

A MASON coming home from lodge met his young son crying his eyes out on the door step. He sat down on the step with him and asked him why he was so upset. The little boy pointed to his bicycle on the lawn which was smashed in two.

"Mummy ran over it in the car." he sobbed.

"Peter, it's your fault if you left it in the middle of the front lawn where she can get at it."

☐

A MASON who was well into his cups was shouting his mouth off at the bar before going into the Festive Board.

"To my certain knowledge," he pontificated, "the Welsh all sing and are either prostitutes or rugby players."

Laughter at the Festive Board

An extremely large barman took offence at this statement and tapping him on the shoulder said:

"Oi, what do you mean by that? My wife is Welsh,"

Seeing the size of the barman convinced him that he would loose any argument where fists were going to be involved, he meekly smiled and said:

"Oh, really, in what position does she play?"

☐

A YOUNG MASON had recently received a brand new Lamborghini car as a twenty fifth birthday present from his parents. He took the car out on the motorway and believing that he wouldn't be hampered by the police (he was on the square) took the car up to 120 mph. A police motorway car eventually stopped him and it wasn't long before he found that his protestation cut no ice with the two policemen.

"I'm sorry, officers, but I think my speedometer must have stuck at 70 mph. Was I going much over that?"

"Well, sir, said the officer writing his driving licence details into his note book "I knew there had to be something wrong. I thought that your altitude metre must have been defective. You were flying much too low."

☐

A MISERLY BROTHER was rumoured to have bought a petrol station. When tackled on this subject by his lodge brothers he was reticent and only gave them evasive answers. However, it became apparent that he had bought it when it was noted that the notice saying "Free Air" had been removed from the station forecourt.

☐

A LODGE was having difficulties in getting new members. They saw their numbers declining rapidly as brethren moved or died. They were persuaded to go to a local prison and to suggest to the governor that any masons currently in prison there could become joining members of the lodge. Their subscriptions were reduced, where the prisoners could not afford the normal fees.

All seemed to go well until a prisoner who became lodge treasurer was found to be in prison for fraud. The counterfeit lodge certificates being circulated made local lodges suspicious.

But, the lodge were admonished when the new secretary sent a lifer to Grand Lodge for the quarterly communications and didn't return.

☐

THE LODGE SECRETARY spent some fifty minutes at the meeting going through the various communications. He sat down somewhat indignantly when he heard a stage whisper from the IPM opposite saying:

"As a secretary he's not bad. As a speaker he is someone who would greatly benefit from catching a large dose of lockjaw or non-infectious laryngitis."

☐

TWO MASONS at their gentlemen's club were reading their evening newspapers when one raised his head and said:

"I was reading a long article in a Sunday magazine about superstition. It is recorded that the most superstitious members of society are freemasons."

"I don't accept that for one minute" said the other. "My uncle was a mason for over forty years and when he broke a mirror he didn't feel that he would suffer seven years bad luck. Of course, he was killed in the same explosion but that's quite incidental."

☐

"BROTHER SAMUEL your delicatessen seems to be doing very well. I am a bit short of funds could you see yourself able to lend me five pounds for a few days?"

"Brother Graham, I regret that as much as I would like to lend you money I have an agreement with Barclays Bank. They have agreed not to sell smoked salmon and cream cheese and I have agreed not to lend money."

☐

ALL LODGE OFFICERS are blue collar workers.

☐

A MASON had aspirations of becoming a benefactor of the Craft. He decided to start a Masonic museum and library at his home. One can only feel for him when he found that while he was away on business his house was burgled and all the books in his library had been stolen. He was particularly incensed by the theft of his books. He hadn't finished reading one and he was only half way through crayoning the other.

> ANY BROTHER SEEN TAMPERING WITH THE MASTER'S CANDLE WILL BE SEVERELY CENSURED. WE ALL WISH THAT THE MASTER'S HAIR AND EYELASHES WILL SOON GROW BACK

© COPYRIGHT GEOFFREY BRYAN 1995

THE BROTHER went up to the lodge secretary and said:

"Excuse me, Worshipful Brother secretary, I am in a bit of an ethical difficulty. I trust your judgement and require your assistance."

"I was in my shop yesterday when a man came in and bought a piece of furniture for £45. He gave me a £50 note and I gave him a £5 note for his change. When I came to put the £50 note in the till I found that there were two notes stuck together."

"My dilemma is this: do I tell my partner or not?"

☐

AN ACTOR was having a drink with the Master of his lodge and was asked how his work was going.

"Well, Master, work has been a bit thin on the ground recently but things really are looking up now. An American TV company is making a thirteen-part adaptation of Robert Louis Stevenson's epic *Treasure Island*. I have been chosen for the main part of the one-legged sea crook 'Long John Silver'."

"I'll be getting £3,000 a week and I start rehearsals on Tuesday."

"For that kind of money I would start rehearsals on Monday." said the Master.

"I can't start Monday. That's the day I'm having my leg off."

☐

THERE WAS a young master, a thunderer,
When his apron were torn asunderer
"I'll get even" he said
"With the newly made head
Of the Regalia shop, who's a blunderer."

☐

THE PRECEPTOR was looking askance
At the newly made master's wild dance
"Oh, you would dance too"
Said his warden "if you
Dropped the rough hewn ashlar by chance."

☐

THE LODGE CHAPLAIN stood with his head bowed
Whilst the lodge sang a hymn very loud
When asked why he did
Said he liked to be hid
As he hated to watch such a crowd.

☐

THE FOOTBALL COMPANY CHAIRMAN took his girlfriend with him to the Ladies Festival and they sat at the table with the team's goal keeper and his wife.

"I don't know very much about football," apologised the bimbo "what exactly do you do as goal keeper?"

"My job is to stop the other team in kicking the ball into my goal."

"You mean those three white posts?" asked the bimbo. The goalie nodded.

"How much does my Brian pay you to do that?" she asked, "more than £500 a week?"

"Twenty times more than that angel." laughed Brian.

"I know you both think me stupid, being a girl and not being a freemason like you two macho men, but wouldn't it be cheaper, in the long run, just to block up the front of the goal with wooden planks?"

☐

STRONG MASONS began to get leery
Of crossing lodge master McCleery
He knew fully the workings
And stepped hard upon shirkings
But the brethren were footsore and weary

☐

A FRENETIC young mason named Plumb
Thought the preceptor really was dumb
His hearty put downs
Made Past Masters clowns
But the lodge thought his actions were rum.

☐

A JUNIOR WARDEN named Bond
Decided to cut short his wand
He drank Martinis well shaken
Cut the fat from his bacon
But his MI5 act had them conned.

☐

CHARITY STEWARDS put it on thick with a trowel.

☐

OLD INITIATES never die, they only change their grips.

☐

TWO SCIENTISTS who attended the same lodge were called by the prosecution as expert witnesses in a murder case. Bill, who was a biologist was called first and gave his evidence and took his seat in the court. Philip a haematologist was called.

"Are you a world authority on blood?" counsel asked him.

"I am, sir" replied Philip without hesitation.

"Would you say that, in fact, you are the major authority in this country on the classification of blood types.?"

"I am sir, the major European authority on the subject."

When the case ended Bill said to Philip:

"Philip, I really was astounded at you in court today. At lodge you keep such a low profile, you are so shy and wouldn't say boo to a goose . Today you threw modesty to the wind, why did you change?"

"Simple, I was on oath to tell the truth," shrugged Philip.

☐

THE BARMAN at the "Flying Ferret" answered the phone to a lady's voice:

"Could you put Bill Jones on the phone, please."

"Sorry, Miss, but there's no one of that name here."

"It's very important that I speak to him. The master of his lodge needs to contact him."

"Sorry, he's not here."

"Well, could I speak to Phil Beaumont. He is always in your pub and he attends the same lodge. He will know where Bill is."

"Sorry, he's not here either."

"This is silly. I know they are both there. Why won't you let me speak to them?"

"Lady, don't give me a hard time. It is the pub's policy that when any lady phones asking to speak to anyone, the gentleman is never here." He replaced the receiver.

Laughter at the Festive Board

◻

CANDIDATES do it irregularly.

◻

PRIOR TO going to his LOI John decided to go to a local pub for a drink. He had never been in this particular ale house and settled down for a quiet drink and to go through his ritual book. After a short time he found that his watch had stopped and went up to a young lady sitting near him and asked her for the correct time.

"How dare you," she screamed, "I am a respectable woman. If you don't go away I'll call the manager."

John went bright scarlet and saw that all eyes in the pub were on him and he tried to calm the young woman down but she just exploded at him again:

"If you say another word I will call the police."

He crept to the other end of the bar and everyone was looking at him with disdain. He had never felt so small and wished for the earth to open.

Within five minutes the young woman came up to him and whispered into his ear:

"I am doing my PhD thesis in Psychology on male re-actions to stress in non-life threatening situations. I hope that you will forgive me for embarrassing you."

John stood up and in his loudest voice said:

"All night? You mean that you'll do that to me all night for only £5?"

◻

AT THE LADIES FESTIVAL the President stood up to make a speech about his long marriage to his darling wife, Sonia, who sat next to him.

"Most people know that I am the owner of a specialised car manufacturing company. We make a particularly popular car and have few rivals because we are so specialised in coach building and cater for the top end of the car market."

─────────────── **Laughter at the Festive Board** ───────────────

"Many people have come up to me and asked me how do I account for such a happy marriage - this year it will be our fortieth wedding anniversary."

"The answer is very simple. I always stick to the one model."

☐

OLD SECRETARIES never die they are usually merely murdered by aggravated lodge masters.

☐

TWO MASON were having a quiet drink after a meeting.

"As a Clinical Psychiatrist at the local hospital, do you specialise in any particular condition?"

"Well, yes I do. I do a lot of work with kleptomaniacs and the reasons why they have the need to steal. I was dealing with one young man who had been a kleptomaniac for many years and after I finished the session told him that he should never find the need to steal again. But, if he did have a relapse it would be appreciated if he would get me the latest Nicam Digital Stereo."

☐

AFTER THE WAR a much decorated Englishman was the guest of a French Military lodge. It was a full dress affair and the Englishman was wearing all his medals including the Croix de Guerre at the Festive Board. As a visitor he was asked to tell the assembled brethren of some of his war experiences. Reluctantly, he stood up and in perfect French related a story about when he was working with the French Resistance.

"To protect one of my lady operatives from a Gestapo officer I had to strangle him with my bare hands. I didn't feel a hero, it was something I just had to do to save a lady's life."

A very attractive young waitress standing near him rushed up to him and before anyone could stop her began to kiss his hands repeatedly saying in French:

"Colonel, let me kiss those hands that have killed to protect the women of France"

She left the room in tears and he, very red faced, resumed his seat.

Laughter at the Festive Board

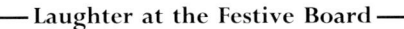

A French captain sitting next to him said:

"You English. You never take advantage of potentially romantic situations. As she was kissing your hands you should have added that you also bit a Nazi to death."

□

THE INCIDENT AT THE LADIES NIGHT

THE PRESIDENT on ladies night
Had much to drink and got quite tight.
His lovely lady tried in vain
To get him to his seat again.

She huffed and puffed to bring him round
The brethren and their wives just frowned
It was not good to see the Master
Looking like a real disaster.

But superman in the guise of Joe,
His IPM, had to have a go.
He lifted Master from the floor
And took him off right out the door.

The room was quietened by the shock
Of Master removed like a sock
But soon they all got back to normal
And all the men looked uniformal.

□

A HAPPY OLD MASON named Bone
Sat in the quiet darkness alone
A candle was lit
Which lightened a bit
But Bone went to sleep on his own

□

A WAND welding warden named Fred
Had a thumping great noise in his head
The initiate's shout
Made old Fred jump about
And he wanded the young man stone dead.

──────────── **Laughter at the Festive Board** ────────────

☐

THE BRETHREN stood upright and square
The master came in with a care
He had broken his leg
Falling over a keg
That should have been delivered elsewhere.

☐

TYLERS do it guardedly.

☐

THE PLATOON of soldiers was waiting in their trench. The young captain took out his revolver and said:

"All right men, wait till you see the whites of the enemy's eyes then let's have some rapid fire."

He was quite taken aback when as the enemy neared the trench five of the platoon started to clap.

☐

OLD MASTER MASONs never die they merely loose the keys to their clarinet cases.

☐

THERE WAS a large audience around the strong man's booth at the local fair. The Great Rudolpho took various strong iron bars which he bent with ease and lifted a bar above his head on which there were large circular weights totalling 200 Kilos as if they were card board. The crowd gasped, clapped and cheered.

He then took a large lemon and with a sharp knife cut it in two. Taking one half he used all his strength to draw out the juice from the lemon. It took him two minutes then he offered the squeezed lemon to his audience and said: "I will personally give ten pounds to anyone who can squeeze another drop of juice from this lemon."

A small elderly gentlemen promptly stepped forward and taking the lemon shell twisted and squeezed it. He gave the lemon one large squeeze and a single drop of juice fell out. The crowd roared their approval.

―――――― **Laughter at the Festive Board** ――――――

"How did you manage to do that?" Rudolpho enquired handing him the ten pound note.

"Well, I haven't been treasurer of a Masonic Lodge for twenty years without learning a thing or two."

AND I HEARD A STILL SMALL VOICE WHICH SAID TO ME 'ROLAND I QUITE AGREE WITH EVERYTHING YOU SAY - THE MASTER AND SECRETARY ARE WRONG — AS USUAL."

©COPYRIGHT GEOFFREY BRYANT 1995

A MIDDLE aged mason had recently gained Grand Lodge honours. He really loved his masonry and asked a Grand Lodge Officer whether he thought that there was a Grand Lodge in heaven and if so how did one get into that Grand Lodge above. The officer said that he didn't know but he knew someone who did and would come back to him on the matter.

The GLO was as good as his word (what else?) and took the mason to one side and said that he had it on the best authority that not only was there a Grand Lodge in heaven but that his Masonic zeal had been noticed by Grand Lodge above and he had been selected to be in that lodge as Grand Junior Warden when he died.

The mason was overjoyed and thanked the GLO profusely but his smile soon turned to anguish when he was then told that there was a meeting the next day and he would be called today to go and get measured for his new collar and apron.

□

THE LODGE bore came up to the lodge secretary. He looked somewhat perturbed and the secretary asked him what was the matter.

55

Laughter at the Festive Board

"Well, Worshipful Brother, John Bloggs has offered me fifty pounds if I would resign from the lodge, What should I do?"

"This is very serious," replied the secretary "but if I were you I would do nothing until he offered a hundred pounds."

"Then what?"

"Take it, my boy, take it"

☐

THE PHONE rang one evening and Bill spoke to the caller.

"It's Joe Smith, the master of my lodge." said Bill to his wife.

He spoke to Joe for about half an hour. When he came off the phone his wife said:

"Do you know, Bill, I wish that I was the master of your lodge. You said 'yes' to him thirty five times during your marathon telephone call"

"I really wish that you were master of my lodge. We change our master every year."

☐

OLD MASONS never die, they only drop their ashlars.

☐

TWO BRETHREN were putting on their regalia before the meeting and the junior brother was helping the other to put his collar on when he spotted that the other was wearing a bra under his shirt.

"How long have you been wearing a bra, Worshipful Master?" he asked with a grin.

"Ever since my wife found it on the back seat of my car."

☐

THE BRETHREN at the final L of I before the Installation had just finished the final installation rehearsal. The Worshipful Brother Preceptor looking very unhappy as he addressed the Lodge:

Laughter at the Festive Board

"Brethren, to say that I am disappointed with you would be an understatement. So few of you officers have learnt your words for tomorrow's installation meeting. Tomorrow we have some very senior brethren attending as visitors and unless you all buck your ideas up, the evening will be remembered as a complete disaster."

"The only brother who has acquitted himself with any honour is brother John, our Master Elect. He is word perfect. He knows where to stand, what to do and from the help he has given the other officers here tonight we can really expect great things of him in his coming year."

Brother John stood up and rather sheepishly took the plaudits offered him and said:

"I thank the Worshipful Brother Preceptor for his kind words. I feel that it is my duty to attend all the LOI 's and to be absolutely word perfect, especially as I won't be able to attend the Installation tomorrow."

☐

THE BARMAN was wiping a few glasses before the evening rush when two pink elephants walked into the bar.

"Sorry lads, you'll have to wait a while. The LOI upstairs hasn't finished yet."

☐

WORSHIPFUL lodge secretary John Bude
Was always a free masonical prude
He pulled down the blind
When he changed his mind
In case cowans and eavesdroppers should intrude.

☐

INNER GUARDS do it pointedly

☐

THERE WAS the case of the Inspector of Taxes who was about to join a lodge until the secretary and treasurer refused their support of his application to join. They realised that this would be difficult for a lodge which was called "Kindness"

57

> BRETHREN IT GRIEVES ME TO TELL YOU ALL THAT OUR BROTHER THE SECRETARY IS GOING TO RETIRE - APPARENTLY HIS QUILL HAS BROKEN AND IT'S THE ONE HE CUT AS A CHILD

© COPYRIGHT GEOFFREY BRYAN 1995

WITH THE number of publicans and policemen in the same lodges I am surprised that not more are called "Firkin and Handcuffs".

☐

TWO EMINENT retired generals were Grand Officers in the Craft and after a most interesting meeting were sitting at the Festive Board when one, leaning back on his chair, with his cigar in his hand said:

"Do you know Ronald, old chap, my son got married last year to a sweet young thing. But her head is made of candy floss or some such light weight matter."

"Why do you say that?" enquired the other.

"Well, when I told her that my great-great grandfather got killed at Waterloo, she asked 'At what platform'?"

"Silly young thing," smiled the other, taking a puff at his Havana "as if it mattered what platform he was killed at."

☐

GRAND RANK OFFICERS never die they always get saluted with three.

☐

A SELF-MADE man became master of his local lodge and had a very high opinion of himself. He had a very haughty manner and many of the younger brethren suffered verbal abuse from him.

On one particular occasion the recently made apprentice was driving down a road near to the lodge which had cars parked on both sides of the road when the master in his large Rolls Royce came into the road from the other end.

Although, the apprentice was only twenty foot from the end of the road the master refused to budge. Sticking his head out of the window he shouted:

"Young man I never back up for idiots."

The young man gave a shrug and shouted out even louder "I always do." And reversed down the road.

☐

SIMON BOLIVAR (The Deliverer) the great South American general and also a great member of the craft was entertaining two English masons. After they had dined Bolivar asked them if they had ever been to a bull fight. The two Englishmen looked very uncomfortable and said that they hadn't nor did they want to.

Bolivar stood up and banged his fist on the table. "You should, my friends, it is my country's first national pastime."

"But its revolting." sneered one of the Englishmen.

"No senor, that is our second national pastime."

☐

MY OWN lodge uses the Taylor workings which aficionados will know started out in lodges affixed to military regiments. Because of this the ritual has a very military feel. Military steps are taken and corners are squared in a military fashion.

I heard that some years ago a junior deacon dropped his wand at an installation meeting and the master's honour guard took him outside and shot him.

☐

WHAT IS the collective term for masons is it a secrecy or a craftiness?

Laughter at the Festive Board

☐

OUR MASTER has worked like two men during his year of office. - Laurel and Hardy.

☐

SENIOR STEWARDS never die they just become Inner Guards.

☐

AN ENGLISH lodge chaplain visited his brother's lodge in Zimbabwe and after the meeting, before the Festive Board was ready he left the lodge room and strolled into the bush. He had not gone more than thirty yards when a huge lion stood in his way. The chaplain was petrified with fear and fell on his knees to pray for help.

At this the lion also went down on his knees, held his paws together, closed his eyes and started to move his lips.

The chaplain's face lit up and he was just about to cry out with thanks when his joy turned to shock horror as he heard the lion gently sing: "For these and all Thy mercies given we love and praise Thy name O Lord."

☐

THE YOUNG mason had joined a local lodge after some years in his mother lodge. Unfortunately, his mother lodge used Emulation workings and the local lodge used Taylor's. He quickly rose to S.W. but had great difficulty in keeping to Taylor's and considered that he 'knew it all' and really hated being corrected by the Worshipful Brother Preceptor at the L.Of I. Indeed, after six weeks he went up to the preceptor and said:

"Look here, old boy. I'm getting rather cheesed off by your constant correction of my words in the ritual. Who do you think you are, my father?"

"I am sorry that you feel that I am getting at you, but my job is to see that all brethren in this lodge keep to Taylor's workings. And, in no way do I consider that I am your father. That I could never be, because, you see, I am married."

☐

AN OBNOXIOUS young man wished to join his brother's lodge. He pushed and bullied his brother and his brother's best friend to sponsor and second him.

"Billy," said his brother, "I would not push this if I were you. I think that even if we get your name put onto the summons the probability is that you will not survive the lodge ballot."

"Rubbish. I insist that you get me in, after all if you don't try I'll tell mother, so there."

His brother did his best and all the normal entry procedures were adhered to and the day of the ballot came and the lodge voted. Afterwards the brothers met.

"Well, how did the ballot go? I did get voted in, didn't I?"

"Well no. When the ballot box was opened I was reminded of the time I kept a herd of goats and had to clean out their pens."

☐

COWANS never die they just never become regular.

☐

IT WAS closing time at the bar of the 'Broken Column Hotel'. The two police officers sat in their unmarked police vehicle in a side road where they had good view of the people leaving the pub. The first man out was swaying all over the place and when he got to his BMW he spent minutes trying to get the key into the lock.

"I think that we've got a drunk in charge here, Billy boy" said the police driver "we will follow him and give him the bag."

"What about the others?"

"Let's concentrate on chummy in the BMW. We can keep him off the road for the next year."

They followed the BMW for four miles but the driving was faultless. The police then pulled him over and said that they thought his back offside light was not working.

The driver protested that his car was in order and denied when asked that he had been drinking anything but orange juice the whole evening.

The breathalyser test proved negative and he agreed to go with the policemen to the station for a water test. This also proved negative and the man was asked by the police to wait while they decided on their next move.

Whilst he was sitting in the waiting room a Chief Inspector passed him.

"Hello, Rupert," said the senior policeman "having a bit of a rest?"

Rupert smiled and nodded.

"Sorry I missed the Installation this afternoon," said the Chief Inspector, "but I've got a stack of work on my desk. Next year I've promised myself that I'll get down to a bit of study and go for office. By the way, did you get anything at the meeting?"

"Yes, as a matter of fact I did. Decoy Deacon."

☐

OUR NEW master is on a fast track so we had casters fitted to his dais.

☐

"I FEEL like telling that swine of a lodge secretary exactly what I think of him again."

"Again?"

"Yes, I felt like telling him it once before."

☐

THE MASON had been sentenced to death for the double murder of his lodge treasurer and secretary who had nagged him about his non payment of both lodge and dining fees.

He continued to protest his innocence from the moment of his conviction and even on the scaffold he pleaded with the executioner, whom he knew to be a well respected member of the Craft.

The executioner was clearly upset and said to the condemned "My brother, I can do nothing for you. You must take this up with Grand Lodge."

"What, the one in Great Queen Street?"

"No, it's to late for that. Take it up with Grand Lodge above. But when I pull the handle be sure to step off with your left foot."

─────────────── **Laughter at the Festive Board** ───────────────

☐

THE THREE lodge members were sitting at a table in the local hostelry when the secretary said:

"The candidate for joining member has three good qualities."

"Firstly, a good ritualise, knows the Emulation ritual throughout."

"Secondly, is extremely rich and will be a large contributor to the charities and the lodge benevolent fund."

"Thirdly, is an excellent organiser and an accomplished after dinner speaker."

'Well, put the name forward." suggested the others.

"Sorry, the candidate has two failings; Firstly, she's an atheist.."

☐

A LODGE treasurer was talking to a brother about the value of money.

"I went through a lot of economics with my young son to teach him the value of money. But I wouldn't do it again."

"Why not?" enquired the other.

"Well, now the young blighter's insisting that I give him his pocket money in Deutschmarks or Japanese Yen."

☐

A MARK MASTER never dies he just fails to make his mark.

☐

A VISITOR to a North Wales lodge was at the Festive Board and was telling everyone how much he had enjoyed the workings. He was ecstatic about the wonderful food and wine being served at the Festive Board.

However, just as the toasts were being announced it was obvious from his words that he wasn't enamoured by one of the senior Grand Officers who was named.

"Unfortunately, I've had business dealings with him and he really has got a face like a sheep's bum."

With that the brother facing him at the table stood up and punched the unfortunate visitor on the nose, knocking him to the ground.

As he staggered to his feet he said:

"I'm sorry if you are enamoured of that man but I speak as I find."

"That was not the reason I struck you, bach " said the enraged brother "this is good Welsh hill country see, and we are very particular how people criticise our sheep."

☐

THE YOUNG mason had recently been made redundant but he managed to get an interview in a firm run by a fellow mason.

At the interview he went through his C.V. and it was obvious from the reaction of his craft brother that he was answering all the questions raised. The interviewer sat back in his chair and said:

"Young man, I am very happy with you and am sure that we would both benefit if you joined us. Only one thing remains - salary. What salary were you thinking of asking?"

"Well, in my last job I was earning £25,000 a year."

"Halve it and you begin", replied the interviewer.

☐

THERE WAS the case of the mason who changed his lodge from one that met four times a year on Saturdays to one that met twelve times a year on Thursday's. He found it so much easier to get away from work than to get away from his wife.

☐

I HEARD of the lodge secretary who had extremely bad handwriting. This would not have been too bad but he went sick just before the lodge meeting. A special committee meeting was quickly convened and it was agreed that they should co-opt the local pharmacist who was in the craft. Apparently, he was the only person able to decipher the secretary's scrawl of the last lodge minutes and read them out to the brethren.

Laughter at the Festive Board

COME TO OUR LADIES FESTIVAL WHERE THOSE WHO CAN'T AFFORD IT MIX WITH THOSE WHO DIDN'T WANT TO ATTEND IN THE FIRST PLACE!!

© COPYRIGHT GEOFFREY BEVAN 1995

THE FESTIVE BOARD was in full swing and the meal was ending and the members and their guests were getting ready for the various toasts and after dinner speeches. Just then one of the entered apprentices started to have violent hiccups. He was offered water, and various patented suggestions to stop his hiccuping but nothing worked.

An old mason of many meetings went over to him and whispered in his ear. As if by magic the hiccuping stopped but the young man still looked pretty ill at ease. The Master went over to the old mason and said:

"How did you cure our young entered apprentice of his hiccups?"

"Very easily, Worshipful Master. I just told the youngster that he was going to give the toast of the Founders and Lodge Officers in five minutes."

□

TWO young masons were rambling through the Yorkshire dales when a mist quickly arose and they found themselves totally lost.

They walked and walked for many miles not knowing where they were or where they were going and just before nightfall found themselves by an eerie ruin.

They walked around the ruin and through the mist found that it was an old lodge hall. Outside of the door of the lodge sat the skeleton of the Tyler with rusty drawn sword. The door of the lodge was now off its hinges but still bore the S and C door knocker.

The went in through the open doorway and found themselves in the lodge. Its carpet now in tatters, the candles all burnt down. The skeletons of the brethren with their badges of blues, silvers and golds still around them.

The masons worked their way around the room and coming to the secretary's table they found the reason for this scene of horror. In front of the secretary's skeletal hand in which lay an old quill pen they saw the lodge minutes.

They read the last words written by the long dead secretary which said:

"OH NO, OUR NEW MASTER HAS FORGOTTEN HOW TO CLOSE THE LODGE AGAIN."

☐

A MASONIC free lance writer was doing a survey of local lodges and the salaries earned by craftsmen from their lodge duties.

He asked MM's, FC's and EA's but none admitted that they benefited monetarily from their lodge attendance.

This was until he asked the lodge organist who said that he earned £30,000 a year from playing the organ. When he was pressed he went to his organ and gave a rousing chorus of "There's no business like show business."

☐

A PRO GRAND CHAPLAIN was called on by the master to reply to the toast of Grand Officers and in his introduction many flattering terms had been given.

In reply he said:

"Thank you Worshipful Master, but I must now say two prayers of forgiveness. First, for you for the many nice lies you told about me. Secondly, for myself for, having enjoyed them so much."

☐

A MASON was coming to an afternoon's meeting. The road was extremely busy and he waited at the zebra crossing when a blind man with his guide dog came by his side.

―――――――――― **Laughter at the Festive Board** ――――――――――

The dog was a lovely Labrador and waited patiently for the traffic to calm down. After a minute or so the dog lifted up his hind leg and peed down the leg of his waiting master.

The man put his hand into his pocket and pulled out a cube of sugar which he held down for his dog.

The mason couldn't help himself and he leaned across to him and said:

"Please don't think me rude, but your dog has just peed down your leg and you are rewarding him with a sugar cube."

"Why don't you mind your own business. I am just trying to locate where his head was so that I can kick him up the bum."

☐

TWO MASONS were returning home from a meeting when, as they approached the house of one of them, a large dog bounded out of the drive way and was hit by the car.

"Oh no," cried one "you've run over Rex. I know that it wasn't your fault, but all the same my wife will be devastated. We must break it to her gently. Just tell her that you ran over one of the children."

☐

THE MEETING was in full swing when one of the distinguished visitors noticed a flea on the blue collar of the Worshipful Master. With a dexterity that defied his eighty years the Pro Grand Master held the offending flea and with his immaculately starched white gloves killed it with a quick pinch between thumb and forefinger.

"Thank you," said the Worshipful Master turning to his protector.

"That's all right old chap. Had to kill him you know, he hadn't been regularly initiated but he had seen and heard too much."

☐

SENIOR LODGE OFFICERS never die they just can't raise their columns.

―――――――― Laughter at the Festive Board ――――――――

☐

WHEN I FIRST joined the craft I thought that "Bread and Butter Masons" were the brethren who did the catering at the Festive Board. At least they would then be doing something useful.

☐

IT WAS going to be the best installation ever if Worshipful Brother Joe, as Master of Ceremonies, had anything to do with it. He would see to it that everything was going to run smoothly.

Those in attendance that afternoon were the assistant Pro Grand Master, his deputy and a visiting American Grand Master.

Joe, had even engaged a world famous soprano to sing "The Master's Song" at the Festive Board.

The afternoon went smoothly. Everyone was word perfect, no promptings were made, it was really a great meeting.

At the Festive Board the stewards all did the lodge, and the new master, proud.

Then came the moment when the diva came out and gave the ever popular "Master's Song". At the end with the clapping loud about her ears came the inevitable cries of "Encore, encore!" She sang again louder and more uplifting than before. Again came the shouts of "Encore". Again she sang and although she smiled and accepted the shouts of the brethren walked to the Master's chair and holding her throat said:

"Gentlemen, as much as I would love to sing 'The Master's Song' again, alas, my throat, it will be too much, I am sorry." She smiled as she turned away.

Joe stood up at once. "Look here, lady, The lodge has paid good money for you. You will sing the damned song till you get it right."

☐

A WELL KNOWN media personality and mason was foliclularly challenged (i.e., bald) and wore a (secret) hair piece. His manager and he went out to Zimbabwe on a working holiday. When it was known to the Harare Television Media his manager was asked if he would care to be interviewed. On the principle that any

Laughter at the Festive Board

advertising is beneficial he agreed that (Worshipful Brother) Peter Smith would appear 'on the box'.

It was extremely hot outside on the day of the live interview and the air conditioning had broken down in the studio. The temperature at the interview was in the high nineties and the six fans just out of camera shot blowing across ice cubes did very little to lower it. They did make a draught which kept the hair piece on the moce.

As the sweat dripped down the face and cheeks of Mr Smith he closed his eyes and wiped his brow with his handkerchief. Unfortunately, he just caught the edge of his billowing hair piece and it floated to the floor by his chair.

His manager, standing just outside of camera range, happened to see the piece by the great man's chair. Being the typical Englishman abroad he was petrified of any creepy crawly and jumped in with both feet. Before anyone could stop him he had totally flattened the black hair piece.

Mr Smith, looked down at the mangled heap of hair, placed his hand to his bald pate, screamed and cried out in anguish.

The public image of Mr Smith depended on his lovely black locks and he had to spend the whole interview with a Panama hat perched tightly on his head.

It was never mentioned about his hat on the T.V. But from then on wherever masons meet Worshipful Brother Smith was known as "Panama" Pete.

☐

A RATHER pompous brother arrived extremely late for the Festive Board after the meeting but although most of the brethren had finished their desserts he insisted on having his luncheon.

"Look," he said to the waiter, "you can keep the first course but I have paid for the meal. I don't want the starter only the main course. I am extremely hungry and I want it hot and I want it now."

"I will do my very best but I think that we may have run out of the main meal."

However, from the look on the newcomer's face he knew that he was beaten. He shrugged his shoulders, nodded and came back in five minutes with a plate of food.

———————— Laughter at the Festive Board ————————

The waiter stood at the door of the kitchen and behind his hand whispered to the Head Chef: "You were right, Francois, I owe you a fiver; the old bugger **has** eaten it."

☐

CANDIDATES are merely hoodwinked into doing it.

GB

"YES, OF COURSE, I LOVE BEING PRESIDENT OF THIS YEAR'S LADIES FESTIVAL BUT I WISH THAT MY DARLING WIFE AND THREE DEAR DAUGHTERS WOULD REMEMBER THAT I'M AN INSURANCE AGENT NOT PAUL GETTY 1, 2 OR 3!!"

© COPYRIGHT GEOFFREY BRYAN 1995

OLD BILL was the oldest member of the lodge and his wife decided that he should have a good holiday in the South of France, where the weather was dependable.

The weather was ideal and they both came back with lovely tans.

Unfortunately, Old Bill was only home two days when he had a heart attack and died.

All the lodge was invited by Bill's wife to say their last farewells to brother Bill whilst he laid in the undertaker's chapel of rest.

As the lodge members filed passed Bill in his open coffin one brother turned to Bill's wife and said:

"That month abroad did Bill a power of good, doesn't he look well?"

☐

THE LODGE CHAPLAIN was also vicar of the local Anglican church. As a community minded man he also ran the Thursday morning assembly at the local girl's high school.

One Thursday morning after assembly the headmistress approached him and asked him what degrees he held. He told her that he had B.A. in Theology and an B.Sc. in Human Biology.

She was delighted and explained that the six form girls were going to have their Human Biology "A" level examination next week but their tutor had gone sick and they needed someone who could give the final lecture. The lecture was going to be on "Sex and Human Reproduction".

The vicar said that he would be pleased to help and gave the lecture.

When he arrived home his wife wondered what had kept him. He knew that she was a bit of a prude and would be less than delighted at his lecture so he told her that the lecture was on "Sailing". She shrugged her shoulders and got on with the dinner.

On the next Saturday the vicar's wife was in the supermarket when she met the headmistress also doing her weekly shopping.

"Would you please thank your husband for that marvellous lecture he gave at such short notice on Thursday."

"I don't know what all the fuss is about. After all, he has only done it three times. The first time he was sick, the second time his hat blew off and the third time he had to be rescued by helicopter."

☐

LODGE TREASURERS never die they just can't be reconciled.

☐

A SECRETARY'S prayer:
Oh, GAOTU, truly blessed are they that hath nothing to say and who cannot be persuaded to say it, S.M. I.B.

☐

SOME MM's are born great, some FC's achieve greatness and some EA's have the toast to Founders, Past Masters and Officers thrust upon them.

☐

AN OLD TYLER whilst testing his sword
Cut the tip off the nose of a Lord
'Hey, look out, I say'
In a nasally way
Or I'll cut off your tassels - by Gawd

☐

AT THE Ladies Festival the elderly mason looked uneasy. He had been a widower for two years now and had decided to support his lodge by coming that evening. He was introduced to a very attractive woman by her brother in law, whom he knew to be in the craft. He got along quite well with her but did not think much of it until he sat down for the meal and found that she was seated on his right.

They talked small talk through the starter but she also shared her talk with her other neighbours to the right and in front. During the main course he felt her left leg press against his. He, without thinking, pressed back. Her leg didn't move but stayed firm. He pressed back harder and still her leg was firm.

She turned to him and smiled and resumed the small talk. He pressed again and was in absolute raptures. Feeling that he had a rapport with her he continued his pressing throughout the meal.

As the coffee and liqueurs were being served he came down with a jolt when she excused herself from the table, but the pressure was still on his leg and he found, to his horror, that he had been pressing against the table leg for the whole of the meal.

☐

THE LADIES NIGHT preparations were in full swing and the lodge secretary was sorting out the prizes for the raffle. His young assistant came up to him and said:

"I've got the list of raffle supporters here. Do you think the new master could run to a bottle of scotch?"

"Run to it? If necessary, our new master would crawl to it."

☐

"YOUNG MAN," said the Master of the lodge, "exactly why do you wish to join the ranks of freemasons?"

Laughter at the Festive Board

"Well, my late father and grandfather were freemasons, as were my late uncles. As I have no brothers I felt that it was my duty to keep freemasonry alive in my family."

"You then are aware of what we in the lodge would expect from you."

"Yes, I know that I should always keep my mouth closed and my ears open. I should forever keep my hand in my pocket and support the lodge, its charities and the annual Ladies Festival. And lastly, if I ever get fed up with the lodge then I know that it is better that I don't attend meetings but not become a country member: Continue to pay all my dues on time and keep whinging like the other brethren."

"Young man," said the stern faced master "with an attitude like that you should be in the chair within the next four years"

☐

A PRO Grand Lodge officer took his small daughter to the circus. They sat in the front seats by the red painted edge of the ring. He found it was very boring but his daughter was laughing and cheering and was enjoying it immensely. Just then a clown with red yellow and blue face makeup came up to them. He did a few funny falls which threw the little girl into hysterics and "splashed" the audience with silver paper in imitation of water. The crowd roared but still the Grand Officer looked bemused.

As he was the only one in the clown's immediate audience not laughing the clown was somewhat unhappy. He went up to the miserable chap and said:

"Excuse me sir, but if you think that you could be funnier then I suggest that you put on funny clothes and show me your act."

"Sir, I regret that I am no music hall clown but if you want to get more material I suggest that you visit Pro Grand Lodge's next Quarterly Communications."

☐

A SILVER service waitress at the Festive Board was serving a young mason who happened to be a well known actor. She stopped serving and stared at him for some seconds.

"I know your face," she said "now where have I seen you before?"

"Could it be at the pictures?" He smiled his chest puffing up.

"That's possible; where do you normally sit?"

THE LODGE TREASURER had been in that position for some twenty years and told both the secretary and the master that he would like to stand down and wanted some younger brother to take over.

As no one in the lodge wanted to take on the job a few arms were bent and a few favours were called in. John, a young mason who had only been in the lodge five years, reluctantly agreed to learn the treasurer's job.

During his first week he learnt about subscriptions and the number of brothers who were in arrears. His second week saw him dealing with the benevolent account at the bank. The third week he was put on reconciling the lodge's current account with cheques received and issued.

John felt that the treasurer was making too much of the difficulty of his position. Of course, the position was important but at the end of the third week John knew it all.

However, he was somewhat surprised to receive a call from the lodge's bankers to say that the current account was overdrawn.

"We just can't be overdrawn at the bank," John told the treasurer, who heard him open mouthed, "I've still got fifteen cheques left in the lodge's current account cheque book."

☐

FREEMASONS do it esoterically.

☐

A MAN walked into a high class confectioners and spoke to the chief patiserier.

"Do you make special celebration cakes?" he enquired.

"Certainly, sir. Exactly what kind of cake are you looking for?"

"Well, here is a very rough drawing of the cake which you see is a pair of compasses and try square on a purple cushion which is edged with a gold fringe."

"Ah, the Masonic symbol. I am sure that we can do that for you."

The patiserier read the measurements from the paper and said that the cake would be ready in two weeks time.

However, when the man called for the cake he was not overly impressed by the colour of the compasses and requested they be coloured bluey silver. The confectioner said that he would attend to that himself and told him that if he called in the next day the cake would be ready.

When he called in as requested he was happy with the colours but thought the cushion could be a little thicker. Again the confectioner told him that he would have the cake alterations made and it would be ready next day.

The cake was ready when the man called. As he paid for the magnificent cake the confectioner said:

"Sir, as the cake is rather heavy we will be pleased to deliver it to your address at no extra cost to you."

"Thank you, but there will be no need. I'll eat it now."

I REALLY LOVE BEING A LODGE CHAPLAIN — AT LEAST HERE I DON'T HAVE THE WORRY OF A WOMAN TAKING MY JOB

© COPYRIGHT GEOFFREY BRYAN 1995

THE LADIES FESTIVAL committee had decided that for the lodge's centenary year they would hold the festival at a really posh hotel. They had arranged with the hotel's management for special rates for brethren and their guests and the allocation of tickets was quickly snapped up.

The new lodge Master and his lady arrived and went quickly to their room so that they could unpack their evening wear. Unfortunately, it was soon evident that the Master's black bow tie was missing and he sent his wife off to the hotel shop to get him one.

On her return he noticed that the bow tie was not the normal clip on with elastic but a "proper" one which neither he nor wife aided could tie up. She went to replace the tie but came back with the same tie. The shop had sold out of clip-ons.

It was too late to go in search of another tie so after he had put all his evening wear on he decided to see if he could find some brother or other who would tie the bow for him.

He went out of the room and a smartly dressed man in evening suit and nicely tied bow passed him.

The Master excused himself and asked him if he would assist him in his quest to tie his tie. The man smiled and said:

"Certainly old chap, but please don't ask me any questions and just do as I ask. Let us go into your room where you must lay down on your bed."

The Master looked quizzically but did as he was bid. His wife looked bemused as only wives can as he laid down.

The helper took no more than five seconds to tie a beautiful professional looking bow and the Master got up from his bed and admired it in the mirror.

"It was extremely good of you to help me out like that but tell me why did I have to lay down for this?"

"Well you see it's part of my job to tie bow ties that way. You see I'm an undertaker."

☐

TREASURERS do it monetarily.

☐

IN SOME lodges aprons with pouches are known as the Australian or Marsupial model.

☐

OUR LODGE has the most wonderful benevolent fund. When you die you don't have to pay any more money into it.

Laughter at the Festive Board

☐

A VERY senior Grand Lodge Officer was sitting behind two masons who were chatting through the whole of the lodge proceedings. At last in desperation he lent forward and tapped one of the men on the shoulder. As the man turned he said:

"Excuse me, but I can't hear a word."

"So I should hope. We sir, are having a private conversation."

☐

AT THE Ladies Festival the master's wife just went into the ladies to remove her beautiful full mink coat when she met her daughter coming out.

"Mother, how could you wear that coat. You know that a poor, dumb creature had to sacrifice everything to provide you with that."

"How dare you, Maureen; that is no way to speak about your father."

☐

THE VISITOR went over to the master as he was removing his collar and apron and was gushing with praise of the afternoon's work. After some minutes the praise turned to out and out flattery. Those near to the master were obviously embarrassed. When the visitor eventually went off the master smiled and said:

"Flattery's all right you know - as long as you don't inhale."

☐

LITTLE BILLY was doing his homework when he looked up and said:

"Mummy, how do buffaloes make love?"

"Darling, what a funny question. You know daddy's a freemason."

☐

THE COUPLE's marriage was going through a very bad patch and to compensate he concentrated more and more on his Masonic work joining several local lodges. He went out five evenings a week to various Lodges of Instruction and meetings.

His wife could take it no more and at breakfast one Saturday morning she tackled him:

"Do you know, I think that you love Freemasonry more than you love me."

Looking up from his newspaper he said:

"I love The Royal Antediluvian Order of Buffaloes more than I love you."

☐

TWO LADIES were discussing their holidays and one remarked that they never went abroad.

"Why don't you like aeroplanes or boats. They are quite safe now, you know."

"No, it's not that. Gerald and I were teetotallers but since Gerald's joined the masons he really has learnt how to drink. I am now very worried that if we went abroad for our holidays I would have to pay duty on him when we came back through Customs."

☐

THE MASTER was having a disastrous year. He just couldn't learn his words, the brethren didn't pay any attention to him, even his IPM looked at him with utter contempt.

At his birthday party his wife brought out his birthday cake with all the candles lit and as he blew them out he shut his eyes and made a wish. But when he opened them he found that he was still master.

☐

AFTER A meeting three masons were getting changed when one of their number a Baptist minister was speaking about the evils of strong drink. One of the masons surprised the other when he said:

"Do you know that within a mile radius of Freemason's Hall in Great Queen Street there are over three hundred pubs and I haven't been in one of them."

The minister nodded his approval, but his friend was puzzled knowing that his friend was a heavy drinker. But he was soon re-assured when his friend added:

"I can't remember its name but I know there's one I haven't been in."

◻

A YOUNG mason got married to a charming girl and at the reception told her that he had two confessions to make to her:

"You see darling, I should have told you before but I am extremely keen on freemasonry and in playing golf. In fact when I am not at lodge or talking about Masonic matters I am playing golf.

She nodded and with a very serious look on her face said:

"Well, I have a confession to make to you. You see I am a hooker."

"Don't worry about that, darling. That's something we can sort out together. Just hold your club with your left thumb pointing down and as you address the ball....."

◻

A VERY senior mason was approached by a Masonic communications circle to give a short talk on the "Influence of The York Masons on English Freemasonry".

He was not all that good at writing speeches and asked his private secretary, who was also in the craft, to write a ten minute speech on the subject.

The young man spent many hours at the library at Freemasons' Hall getting information which he compressed into a speech.

On the day of the meeting he gave the speech to his boss who went off and gave the speech.

Next day his boss called him into the of Office and really tore him off a strip:

"I've never had a more unhappy time at a meeting. I'll never be able to show my face there again. My reputation as a speaker is now in ruins. I can't understand what you did to me. The speech was all right at first but became so boring and lasted half an hour. I told you what I wanted didn't I ? What went wrong?"

"I can't understand it, I wrote the speech which you requested and thought that it was interesting and to the point. I know your speed of delivery and estimated that it should only have taken you ten minutes to deliver. As usual I gave you the speech with two carbon copies..."

☐

LODGE CHAPLAINS do it prayerfully.

☐

CHARITY STEWARDS never die they only loose their covenants.

☐

GRAND OFFICERS never die they just let their aprons fade to a lighter blue.

☐

A GRAND LODGE officer was a visitor to a friend's installation and after it told the new master that he would very much like to attend their next lodge of instruction. The master arranged with the lodge secretary for him to attend.

A week later the master was somewhat taken aback to receive a rather curt letter from the visitor saying that although he enjoyed the way the rituals were being taught he was somewhat taken aback by the in-hospitality of the members by not being offered a cup of tea when the lodge closed for refreshment.

The master tackled the man in charge of the LOI the evening in question.

"Gerald, is it true that you didn't even offer the visitor a cup of tea? What has happened to lodge hospitality?'

"I'm sorry, Worshipful Master, but be fair, he wasn't in the kitty, was he."

☐

SERGEANT SMITH was most imposing in the witness box. His thirty years in the craft together with his years in the police force had given him the assurance that he needed to do his job well.

Counsel asked him to give details of exactly what the defendant had said on the night in question.

The sergeant then for ten minutes related, without benefit of his notes, exactly what had been said.

After this time counsel looked at him and said:

"The court is impressed by your performance. Not only did you repeat a conversation word for word without looking at your notes, the conversation took place some nine months ago. It would appear, officer, that you are not as other men and have a first-class, even a photographic, memory. Is that so?"

"That is correct. When I hear anything or see things in print once I can recall what I hear or see immediately and remember it forever."

"Come, come, officer, are you really asking this court to believe that you can remember everything that you have seen or heard?"

"That is correct, sir."

"Can you tell the court something you recall from even further back?"

"Certainly, sir....Hickory dickory dock...."

□

THE MASONIC COMMUNICATIONS CIRCLE was having their quarterly meeting and the secretary had engaged a Deputy Assistant Pro Grand Master to give a speech.

However, there was a disappointing attendance with only five members.

The speaker was incensed and said to the secretary:

"Did you tell the members that I would be speaking tonight?"

"No, but believe me master I'm going to find out who did."

□

GRAND OFFICERS never die, they only forget to attend the Quarterly Communications.

□

OLD DEACONS never die they just forget to turn the tracing boards.

□

DURING WORLD War II a sentry was standing guard outside a military installation when he was approached by a colonel, who should have known better, but decided to have a bit of fun with him.

"Halt, who goes there?"

"A friend."

"Advance friend and be recognised. Give me the password."

"I was taught to be cautious."

"So was I mate. But if you don't want to talk with a high pitch in your voice you will give me that password freely and at length."

□

BRIAN AND ROBERT had just been to a meeting and had thoroughly enjoyed the liquid element of the Festive Board. They hailed a taxi and when they had got to Brian's house Brian insisted that Robert should come in for a single malt night cap

However, when they came to the front door Brian had great difficulty in getting his key out and when he did his hand was shaking so much he couldn't hit the key hole.

"I'll tell you what, buddy of mine. I'll hold your hand to steady it, OK?"

"No thank you Robbo, I'll hold the key you just hold the door frame and try and keep the house from moving."

□

THE NEW MASTER of the lodge had a word with the secretary who was also his GP. From the conversation it was obvious to the doctor that the master was suffering from acute anxiety. He suggested that the master spend a few weeks on a farm run by two friends of the doctor.

The master spent the first weeks just lazing about and by the beginning of the third he felt so much better he asked for something to occupy him. He was shown how to drive the tractor and how to get the harvest in.

However, the doctor received a call from the friend saying that the master had had a relapse. He rushed down to the farm and saw the master in his bed rolled into a foetal ball.

"This is extremely serious. Tell me what happened to get him into this state."

"Well, after we showed him how to drive our tractor we got him to help get the harvest in. When he had finished that we sent him into the barn to sort the big potatoes from the smaller ones."

"Oh no," said the doctor, "you mean you actually asked him to make.....decisions?"

☐

TWO MASONS were having a quiet drink before the Festive Board when one said to the other:

"My wife buys her clothes from Marks and Spenders and must spend about two thousand pounds a year there. I wouldn't mind so much but she doesn't take care of them just throws them down in the bedroom and leaves me to pick them up and put them onto hangers."

"Well, I suppose that I am very lucky. My wife is so particular with hers that some days when I come home from work early I've often found a man in her wardrobe standing guard over them."

☐

A TYLER broke his sword which belonged to the lodge. He took it into a Masonic regalia shop to get it mended but lost it on the bus coming home. He reported the loss to both the master and secretary. "I'm sorry Worshipful Brother Tyler but that sword was given to the lodge by a distinguished founder and you will have to replace it. A comparable sword will cost you £250. "

"It's no wonder then that in the British Navy the captain always go down with his ship," sulked the Tyler

☐

"MAUREEN, we must ask Joan and Phil and you and Graham round for an evening meal in the very near future. Perhaps you will help me to do a curry and rice with all the chappatis and chutneys."

"I'd be glad to help but last time we did this it took us both two hours to clear up in the kitchen. The men, who didn't lift a hand to help preparing the food just sat back and let us clean the pots and pans."

"But, Maureen, that was before our men joined the Masons."

"What's that got to do with them clearing up in the kitchen?"

"Well, they tell us that when they wear their aprons. It's only when fellow masons are present. What could be a better time for them to get off their bottoms and put on their aprons if it's not for cleaning and washing up after a good meal."

A POOR MAN, who's wife died, went to a funeral director he knew to be a freemason. He thought that he would get a headstone carved for nothing.

THE NEWLY MADE mason came out of the lodge room and began to tidy himself up. As the Tyler helped him put on his coat there was a gentle tap on the door facing the lodge door. The Tyler went and opened it and found a beautiful young lady in a very low cut blouse and short skirt. Thinking that she was just a waitress wanting to prepare the lodge room for the Festive Board he said:

"I'm sorry, my dear, but I'm afraid that you are about two hours too early. You will have to come back then..."

He was interrupted by the candidate who said:

"That's all right, she's with me. She's the personal comforts that are to be returned to me after my initiation."

◻

SOMETIMES IN the craft a mason may get carried away with his charitable given. Such a mason's wife was looking at a statement of their joint current account and said:

"Darling, you seem to be spending quite a bit of money on that lodge of yours."

"I know, dearest, but I have to support the Broken Column you know."

"By all means support it but the way you've been giving you could have repaired all the columns at the front of the British Museum by now."

◻

AN OLD miser had been in the craft for over forty years. Unlike his lodge brothers he found it difficult to give either to his lodge's benevolent fund or to the charities.

At the age of seventy he died and stood by the pearly gates for some time until St Peter and St John the Baptist, the patron saint of his lodge, came out. St Peter had a long list which he looked through. St John asked if anything was wrong. St Peter looked up and said:

"This miserable creature, a member of your illustrious lodge, has in his Masonic career only given four pounds ninety five pence to charitable causes. What shall we do?"

"Give him a fiver and tell him to go to Hell." Said St John with a sad smile.

◻

DURING THE French-Indian Wars fought in eastern Canada in the eighteenth century a young British Officer was captured by Iroquois Indians loyal to the French.

Because the officer fought so well the Iroquois wanted to have his courage and as was their custom tied him to a tree and cut the veins in his left wrist and drank his blood. They ensured that they only drank a little as they did not want to kill him.

After he had been tortured this way for some days he could take it no more and cried out:

"You heathens are like some of my Masonic brethren who can't pay their bills at the Festive Board. They are always sticking me for the drinks."

☐

OLD MASTERS never die, they simply lose their aprons.

☐

DEACONS do it with a sweep of their wand.

☐

DURING THE bad days of the blitz many London lodges were damaged by bombs and incendiaries. One such lodge which met over a public house was hit after all the members had gone down to the shelter. When the lodge resumed it was their hall that was lacking a roof and two walls. Nevertheless it was agreed to carry on but the lodge members fell about when the Inner Guard answered the Tyler and turning said:

"Brother Junior Warden, there is a report."

Coming in fast the IPM said "Yes, and a bloody big one at that."

☐

IT HAD been a rather acrimonious lodge meeting and there was some argument between the lodge treasurer and one of the lodge auditors. It got rather heated and the treasurer said:

"Brother Simpson is the most pigheaded idiot I have had the misfortune to meet."

Hoping to calm the situation the master knocked with his gavel. "Brethren, brethren," he shouted," you both seem to forget that I am here."

☐

A MASON, who wanted to be the lodge secretary could hardly contain his delight when he heard that the secretary had had a massive heart attack and died.

He immediately telephoned the master and said:

"I'm so sad to hear that our Worshipful Brother Secretary has died but I would be very pleased to take his place. Do you think that there might be a chance?"

"Possibly, my boy, possibly. If it's all right by the undertaker then it's all right by me."

☐

THE LODGE MASTER's rule for survival:

> When in doubt, mumble,
> when in trouble, delegate,
> when in charge, ponder.

☐

A TYLER died and as a good Tyler should he went straight to Heaven. At the Pearly Gates he met St Peter who checked that he was on the list. St Peter asked him what he had last been on earth.

"Why I was a Tyler," he replied, somewhat mystified.

"Great. Your just the man I can trust. Look after the gates for a couple of minutes I'm dying to go to the toilet."

☐

A VERY senior mason had a bit of a shock (some one asked him to pay for a round after LOI) and he went grey overnight.

He was extremely upset at this but was persuaded, by his wife, to go to the local hairdresser to see what could be done for him.

"What have you got for grey hair" he whispered to the hairdresser.

"Only the greatest of respect, sir," the hairdresser whispered back.

☐

AT THE end of the meeting the brethren retired to the hotel bar so that the lodge stewards could prepare the room for the Festive Board. One of the visitors began to drink rather heavily and was somewhat the worse for wear when the brethren took their respective places at their tables.

Laughter at the Festive Board

Half way through the meal the visitor was most of the way through a bottle of white wine and he began to get abusive with his neighbours. A steward rushed up to calm him down when the visitor stood up waving his bottle in the air overbalanced and hit the floor with an almighty bang. There was blood everywhere and the master rushed up and said to the young steward who was leaning over the prone brother:

"Good God steward, what's happened. Where is he bleeding from?"

The steward shrugged his shoulders and said:

"I dunno master, but I fink 'e he lives locally."

☐

THE LODGE was going through a quiet period and whereas they normally were doing a "First" and a "Second" or perhaps the long "Third" each meeting they had difficulty in doing a "First" because of the lack of candidates.

"Well, Worshipful Master," said the secretary are you going to do the "Second" or going to get a speaker to do some aspect of Masonic hi
story that might be of interest to the brethren?"

"Yes, I will do the "Second" but I will get W Bro. Jones to give the second degree charge."

The meeting went well and Worshipful Brother Jones went through the Charge like a hot knife going through butter. He got to the piece which says: "forty and two thousand Ephraimites.." He paused and said to the master:

"Would you be pleased to take the names as read, Worshipful Master?"

☐

BILL WAS well known as the lodge poseur and had to present his papers at his local police station and to provide full details of an accident. The sergeant was his lodge treasurer.

"Look Bill, I don't think I can help you here. The accident boys have measured your skid marks and they confirm that you were speeding."

"Absolute rubbish" said Bill.

"Well, what gear were you in?"

"I don't see what that's got to do with anything. But all right..a brown leather jacket, Levi 501's and light tan cowboy boots."

☐

A PRECEPTOR was renowned for his army style ways with the Lodge of Instruction brethren. He was out for a Saturday night drink when he met a lodge brother and they had several drinks together.

After they had a great deal of drink the preceptor said:

"Harry, dear boy, I know that when I die you would like to tinkle on my grave."

"No Bill, you've got me all wrong. Nothing would allow me to do that. I hate to stand in long queues - even for pleasure."

☐

REMEMBER THAT old Masonic quip. The secretary of the lodge is the backbone whereas the Master is only the wishbone.

☐

PRECEPTORS do it instructively.

☐

SECRETARIES do it scriblingly.

☐

GEORGE, one of the lodge's past masters, had sent an apologies for absence note to the secretary. After the meeting the Master rang him at home to see if he was all right.

"I'm sorry, Worshipful Master, but I'm feeling a bit depressed. I've been having tests at the hospital and the doctor called me into his surgery this morning with the results. It appears that I've got some illness that means I must take a little white tablet every day for the rest of my life."

"That's not too bad, George, you should be able to cope with that inconvenience."

"Oh, I can cope with that. The only thing that's worrying me is that the quack has only given me four tablets."

> WORSHIPFUL BROTHER PRECEPTOR — IF I'M NOT SUPPOSED TO SAY "ET CETERA" WHY DO THEY PRINT "ET CETERA" IN MY LITTLE BLUE BOOK ???
>
> © COPYRIGHT GEOFFREY BRYAN 1995

A MASON, who was also a politician, spoke to his secretary at lodge and asked how he might get onto the TV programme "Question Time". The secretary had been in the TV media and knew a few producers and suggested that he wrote to one of them quoting his (the secretary's) name. He mentioned that the fee would be £50.

The producer of "Question Time" was not surprised to get the request for the politician to appear on the show but he was surprised to receive the politician's personal cheque for £50.

☐

HOW MANY in the craft have looked with awe at that part of the Installation ceremony when the Tyler comes in to receive his collar and sword? He does a complicated twist of his wrist and the razor-sharp blade whistles left and right. In our lodge you can always see the masons who habitually sit either side of the Tyler (or D'Artangnon as we in the lodge like to call him) when he comes in. These brethren either have parts of their ears or noses missing or they have permanent twitches waiting for those deadly sweeps.

Some brethren have joined the Templars and have taken to bringing their own swords with them at Installations only if it is to at least protect themselves.

Laughter at the Festive Board

☐

THE LODGE SECRETARY approached a brother, who for many years had wanted lodge office.

"We are currently looking for a treasurer."

"I understood that you only recently filled that vacancy."

"We did, he's the one we are currently looking for."

☐

PAST MASTERs are called upon to do it at a moment's notice.

☐

SOME YEARS ago a certain prelate, who, in public was vociferous against the craft and its members, had his arm twisted and decided to attend a Ladies Festival.

Whilst he was about to dine he was asked by the Toast Master if he would like to say the Grace. He smiled and shook his head and said that he had to decline as he didn't want God to know that he was there.

☐

AS HAPPENS in lodges which are centuries old the brother chosen to give the toast of the Founders finds great difficulty in finding new information on the subject.

A young MM stood up and said:

"It has fallen to me to make the most important toast to the Founders this evening. I feel a bit like wise King Solomon in all his glory when he went to his harem. Seeing his hundred wives and his four hundred concubines said that he knew what to do but how could he make it interesting."

☐

WHEN A MASONIC SPEAKER was asked how he timed his speeches he said that he stood up when they nudged him and sat down when they pulled his coat.

Laughter at the Festive Board

☐

IT IS said that the rules for any private speaking (but especially Masonic after dinner speaking) are:

> Stand up
> Speak up
> Shut up

☐

ALMONERS do it benevolently.

☐

STEWARDS do it at the Festive Board.

☐

A MIDDLE-AGED man went to his doctor and complained about having constant migraines. The doctor referred him to a specialist in Harvey Street and after numerous tests the specialist told him what was wrong.

"From the tests you have the onset of an on-going brain disorder. It can't be cured but with today's technology you can have brain transplant."

The man asked to see what brain he could have if he decided to go through with a transplant.

He was shown first a brain in a liquid filled tank which had a sign marked £5,000. "This was the brain of a top scientist and is well worth that sum."

The second brain he was shown was marked £10,000. "'The brain of a first class surgeon. A superb specimen I am sure you will admit and a snip at the price."

They came to the third tank in which there was a beautiful specimen, this time with a price label of £30,000.

"That's a hell of a lot of money for a brain, isn't it?"

"Certainly not," replied the consultant indignantly, "this brain was once owned by a lodge treasurer, it really is in tip top condition - never been used you see."

POLICEMEN WHO ARE ALSO LODGE OFFICERs never die they only get their collars felt.

☐

AT THE end of the speech making the lodge ladies festival chairman thanked all those attending that evening. He said:

"In some lodge only half of the committee works extremely hard - the other half does nothing. I'm glad to say that here it is the other way around."

☐

WORSHIPFUL BROTHER Fred was a well liked mason. He supported all the lodge functions and, it has to be admitted rather liked the liquid refreshment offered at the Festive Board. After an installation he went off with the new master and the IPM and several others and did the round of pubs and clubs in the West End of London. His fatal mistake was in not telling his wife who was waiting up for him when he returned home at 11.00 next morning.

"Where the hell have you been?" she shouted at him as he staggered in, hands holding his throbbing head.

"You know where - I've been to lodge," he whispered.

"What, till eleven in the morning? Come off it Frederick."

"Look, dearest heart, no need to shout. One of the brethren put me up as it was getting late". He would take no more questions and went straight to bed.

His wife, being the dutiful wife of a freemason, wasn't going to leave it there and next day took out Fred's lodge summons and got the names and addresses of all the brethren from the back page. Using her word processor she produced a merge letter which simply asked each of the thirty lodge members to confirm that Fred had spent the previous night at their house. She put a stamped addressed envelope in each one, posted the lot and sat back waiting for the replies. When she eventually received all the replies she was shocked to receive thirty "Yes's"

☐

DEACONS do it with their wands.

THE LODGE SECRETARY was having a disastrous meeting. He dropped his spectacles and broke one of the lenses of his reading glasses, knocked over his water glass and then showered the lodge with his papers including all the communications from Grand Lodge and Provincial Grand Lodge.

He gathered all his precious papers just as he was called by the Master to stand and give the lodge the various details of the communications.

In a hoarse whisper to his Assistant Secretary he said:

"What should I take next, Bill?"

"Try poison, Worshipful Brother Secretary."

TWO OLD 'gentlemen of the road' (tramps to you and me) were in Trafalgar Square eating a light repast when one turned to the other and said:

"Dick, how is it that I'm as poor as a church mouse but you always seem to have a few quid spare in your pocket?"

"In this life you've got to use some nowse. Once a week I go to the Freemasons' Peace Memorial - that's Freemasons' Hall to you - and wait near to the side door. When a large chauffeur driven car draws up and a man gets out wearing a dark suit and a black tie and carrying a small brown or black clarinet case I walk up to him. I touch my forehead and say:

"Help a poor and distressed Freemason. The bloke has to give me something, it's part of their religion."

"Blimey, if its that easy I'll go tomorrow."

The next day he was waiting by the side door of Freemasons' Hall when he saw a large black limousine draw up. A tall distinguished Grand Officer got out. His ritual case was twice the size of the clarinet case that the tramp was expecting.

"Spare a copper for a poor and distressed Freemason, yer Lordship, sir?"

The Grand Officer looked at the down at heel man and said:

"A poor and distressed Freemason, eh."

"Yes, your honour."

"Before I will give you something I feel that I should ask you a question. What comes after '* *'?"

The tramp shrugged and answered "Whitechapel?"

"No, no," said the Grand Officer in exasperation," * and *, or if you prefer *,*"

"Cheers mate. Look here, you wouldn't smell too marvellous if you'd spent the last two, years sleeping rough. You can keep your handouts if all you can do is insult me."

☐

OLD MASONs never die they can't knock off their superfluities

☐

TYLERS do it gladiatorially

☐

A BROTHER went up to Scotland on business. He was asked by his Scottish business associate if he would like to attend a meeting the next day. The Englishman was delighted and really enjoyed the workings. He asked his Scots brother whether there was any chance of playing golf at the weekend. The Scotsman said that they should play at his club. He added with a wry smile and a twinkle in his eye:

"Let's play for a small wager - £10 a hole."

The Englishman had had too many 'wee drams' to do anything but agree. The next day at the Golf course the Englishman teed off and after he had finished the first tee the Scotsman asked:

"Well, brother, how many strokes did you take."

"Six," replied the sassenach.

Laughter at the Festive Board

"I only took five. That makes it my hole."

At the second the Englishman again teed off and at the end the Scotsman asked the same question:

"How many strokes."

"Five this time."

"Bad luck, I only took four. My hole again."

The third was a dog leg and took twice as long to complete.

"Well, laddie, how many strokes this time."

"Just a minute, Jock, Play fair, I think its my turn to ask first."

☐

IT HAS been said that the best after dinner Masonic audience is:

One, intelligent. Two, well-educated. And three, more than a little drunk.

☐

THE PRESIDENT of the ladies festival stood up and said:

"To all the gentlemen here I will divulge a piece of information that will stand you in good stead with any lady. It comes from Oscar Wilde who said: "As long as a woman can look ten years younger than her own daughter, she is perfectly satisfied."

☐

> **A CERTAIN** lodge Master named Fred
> Could not keep the words in his head
> The preceptor, his brothers
> And a lodgeful of others
> Tried prompts but he'd lost his lodge cred.

☐

THE LODGE's junior warden was selected to attend quarterly communications but on the day felt a bit under the weather and phoned his lodge secretary to tell him that he could not attend. The secretary obviously was less than happy at this but as there was no one who could go at such short notice had to attend himself.

The junior warden decided to go down and play a round of golf at his local course. It was a lovely day but even without the pressure of a partner he was taking 8 to 12 strokes a hole.

Looking down on him from on high were the Heavenly Grand Officers.

"That young man should be punished. Telling lies like he has to get him off doing his Masonic duties."

The other smiled and waved his hand just as the junior warden teed off and the ball this time was neither hooked nor sliced but accurately hit the flag and went into the hole. The legendary 'Hole In One.'

"But, Master, you have rewarded him."

"He is being punished. Who can he tell back at the lodge?"

A VISITOR to the lodge was chosen by the secretary to respond to the toast of 'The visitors' and was looking decidedly ill at ease at the Festive Board. He was going over and over his notes.

The secretary leaned over and said:

───────────────── **Laughter at the Festive Board** ─────────────────

"Look lad, don't be getting yourself too worked up about the speechifying. Remember the one rule of Masonic speech making: they don't expect much."

□

GRAND LODGE does it by communicating quarterly.

□

OLD LODGE SECRETARIES never die they simply fail to dip their quills.

□

A NAIVE young mason went to his weekly lodge of instruction with a very black eye. All the brethren looked up as the preceptor said:

"What happened to you brother Robert? Walked into a door?"

"No, I got it last Sunday at church. I was sitting down when a very large lady in a light summer frock sat down in front of me. It was all right until we all stood to sing a hymn then I noticed that her frock had got caught in the cleft of her bottom. I reached over and gently pulled it out. She turned around and punched me in the eye."

"Bad luck Robert, but I'm sure that you've learned your lesson and won't do that again."

On the next LOI Robert came in this time with his other eye black and blue and before being asked by anyone he said to the assembled lodge:

"Before you lot ask I was at church last Sunday and the same lady came in wearing the same frock. When she got up to sing a hymn the frock again was caught in the cleft of her bottom. I knew better than to touch it. However, the man next to me leaned over and gently pulled it out. I knew that she didn't want that so I pushed it back into the cleft with my fingers."

□

THE LADIES FESTIVAL was in full swing when the daughter of the current master was in the ladies rest room combing her hair.

"Pauline, how lovely to see you again," said the wife of the IPM, "back from that finishing school in Switzerland I see. Such a shame you missed Harold's Ladies Festival last year, it was truly magnificent. Do you know that when I made the speech for the ladies I was clapped for a full ten minutes."

"Fantastic." smiled Pauline.

"Yes, and the whole lodge paid for a gorgeous gold and diamond bracelet that must have cost them two thousand pounds, at the very least."

"Fantastic." smiled Pauline.

"Yes, and I have been invited personally by the wife of the Pro Grand Master of ….shire to form a Masonic Ladies Circle."

"Fantastic." Smiled Pauline for the third time.

"By the way, Pauline, what did they teach you at your Swiss finishing school?"

"Oh, they taught me to say 'fantastic' instead of 'bull sh*t'."

☐

TWO OPERATIVE MASONs were having their high twelve repast when one said to the other:

"Brother Will, how long have we been working on this cathedral? Is it six or seven years now?'

"Can't rightly say Brother Bernard, but I think it could be seven years last Michaelmas. Why do you ask?"

"Well, when we started I thought that we were here to build a castle for the duke."

"So did I, but it's the same the world over; another Master in charge who has a little bit of trouble understanding what the work for the year should be."

☐

ROBERT HAD been a lodge member for thirty years and from the way he conducted himself and the way he dressed was known as the lodge slob. On a hot Saturday in lodge during a 'First' he had a mild heart attack. A brother, who was a doctor, looked after him and got him to hospital. When he was better the brother read him the riot act and told him that if he wanted a long and fruitful life he had to take better care of himself.

Robert was truly frightened by his ordeal and taking the advice of his lodge brother went on a strict diet - no booze or fatty food. He exercised every night and morning. As he got better he took a good look at himself and decided that he would not go back to his old lifestyle but promised himself to change his old sick image.

He threw away his glasses and bought contact lenses, a toupee and with his new slimmer self he bought trendy suits.

Everyone in the lodge was extremely pleased with the fact that Robert not only had completely recovered but that he looked so well. He even took lodge office, something that he had always declined. He gave freely to all the Masonic charities.

When he got to the chair within two years he planned out his whole year with the secretary and was looking forward to his first full meeting. He died that evening.

Arriving in Heaven he went up to the recording angel and said:

"Look, I really pulled myself up by my boot straps, took a good look at myself and I was really looking forward to being master of my lodge and you bring me up here before I am ready."

"Oh, it is Robbo, isn't it? Robbo, I'm so sorry I just didn't recognised you."

☐

MANY BRETHREN have enough masonry to make them decent but not enough to make them dynamic.

☐

AT THE Ladies Festival several ladies were in the powder room when one of them looked into the mirror and as she mascared her eye lashes she remarked:

"I only admit to being forty nine. I don't care if that makes my son, the current master, illegitimate."

"I wouldn't worry darling, most of the lodge think he is anyway."

———————— **Laughter at the Festive Board** ————————

☐

TWO MASONs were taking off their regalia after the meeting.

"Don't you wish, Philip, that you could still do all the things that you did when you were seventeen?"

"Daniel, when you are my age you can do all the things that you could do when you were seventeen. That's if you don't mind making a complete plonker of yourself."

☐

THE OLD mason was having a quiet drink with a young apprentice. He look at the tall sprightly young man and smiled:

"As time goes by you tend to slow down and replace the active games you used to play for the even more active game; called hunting for the spectacles to find the summons. You will even find tying the apron snake buckle gets to be quite a feat in itself. So if you would be forever looked up to in the lodge just look after a doddering old mason. You can draw the line, though, at cutting up his dinner at the Festive Board and wiping his mouth for him."

☐

TWO OLD masons decided to join a safari in Kenya. They both enjoyed, with all the others, taking photographs of the scenery and the wild animals in their own environment.

However, as they were intent on taking photographs they found that they had become separated from their group. As they started to find their way back to the camp site they saw to their horror a large lion. They looked at each other and one said:

"Let's run for our lives."

"But we can't run very fast. You've got arthritis and I'm over eighty. We'd never outrun that brute."

"Sorry, Fred but I don't have to run very fast. Only a little bit faster than you."

☐

OLD LODGE STEWARDS never die their horns of plenty just run dry.

THE PROVINCIAL Grand Lodge decided to hold a GRAND CHARITY BALL to help the poor and homeless in the county.

It turned out to be a brilliant occasion and everyone who attended had a fantastic time.

As the ladies and gentlemen all dressed in their finery left the ball a rather superior lady in tiara and jewellery was getting into her Rolls Royce when a dirty old tramp put his hand on her arm and begged for some small change.

The superior lady looked at his dirty hand on her and said:

"You dirty ungrateful fellow. You have no idea, have you? I've been wearing myself out, dancing myself silly all night for the likes of you."

☐

REMEMBER THAT a compliment paid in the lodge may just be the right amount of soft soap that can wipe out a dirty look.

☐

PHYSICALLY THE tongue is only three inches from the brain, but when you listen to some masons in lodge these two organs seem many miles apart.

☐

UNFORTUNATELY, in Masonry, as in other disciplines a nugget sized brain is often made up for by a bucket sized mouth.

☐

WHEN IT is said that a brother is a "born mason" it may just mean that his old dad was a founding father.

☐

A GOOD lodge secretary has inborn ability or talent for deciding something quickly and getting someone else to do it but let the master believe that it was his idea in the first place.

Laughter at the Festive Board

☐

IF YOU would like to hear all about the troubles in the lodge, ask a brother who hasn't been there for several months.

☐

THE MOST expensive seat in any lodge is the seat of an absent brother.

☐

THE WILFUL absence of a brother from lodge is the first vote to close the lodge.

☐

LODGE ATTENDANCE is determined more by desire than by distance.

☐

A GOOD lodge secretary is not necessarily smarter or cleverer than others in the lodge. He has just got his ignorance better organised.

☐

THE BEAUTIFUL young lady at the ladies festival was just putting her lovely mink coat into the cloakroom when she spotted a girl friend and hugging her said:

"Hi, Susan, fancy meeting you here. Who are you with tonight?"

"Oh hi, Joanne. Only Johnny my fiancee. Who's your beau for tonight?"

"Why, I'm with the Worshipful Master. He's a wonderful man and last week he took me up to his bedroom and in his walk-in wardrobe he's got ten fur coats. He gave me the one I'm wearing tonight."

"Oh, yes. What did you have to do for that?" smirked Susan.

"Only shorten the sleeves." shrugged Joanne.

☐

THE VICAR of the parish became chaplain in his lodge. He found it very dificult to get on with his brother masons who were all rather boorish.

He was having a quiet sherry with a brother from a different lodge when the brother said:

"Father John, when you have to say a prayer in lodge who do you pray for, the brethren?"

"Oh no. When I see the brethren I pray for the lodge."

> BRETHREN OUR IMMEDIATE PAST MASTER HAS TAKEN WINE WITH HIS BROTHER THE CHARITY STEWARD - THE POLICE EXPECT TO MAKE AN EARLY ARREST

© COPYRIGHT GEOFFREY BRYAN 1995

BEFORE HE went to the Festive Board one of the brethren had already been drinking heavily. At the table he had drunk one of the bottles of wine before the first course was over. He had misbehaved with the silver service waitress as she took away the dishes. When she returned with the dishes for the main course he again tried to get familiar. One or two of the brothers spoke to him about letting the lodge down but he was too drunk to care. When the waitress laid the meat on his plate he picked up a slice of meet with his fork and said to her:

"Oi, darlin', is this pig on the end of me fork?"

"At which end, sir?"

□

AN ELDERLY senior member of the lodge had his eighty fourth birthday whilst he was at lodge. The brethren arranged for a beautiful birthday cake to be made.

The cake was brought in at the Festive Board which was reserved for the dessert.

Laughter at the Festive Board

The cake was clapped in by the brethren and the birthday boy smiled but then seeing that there were no candles on it he asked why.

"Worshipful Brother Ted, all your friends here wish it to be a really memorable time for you. It was decided not to put candles on the cake and light them. Although it was your birthday we didn't want to turn it into a torch light procession."

☐

WE ONCE had a master who was a really big man. Why the Polaroid snap of him in full regalia weighed over six pounds.

☐

AN OLD LADY was being shown around Freemasons Hall. She was shown the Masonic museum and the library and then shown the Temple.

She looked in awe at the beautiful colours of the magnificent columns. The gilding were superb.

"Just think, young man," she said to her guide, "what this place must have looked like when King Solomon was here."

☐

KING SOLOMON is a man much venerated in our rituals for his foresight and strength of character. But, how many of us really have given much thought to how unhappy a man he must have been. Not only did he have a hundred wives nagging him all night in bed he had a hundred mothers in law nagging him in his palace all through the day. It is litttle wonder that the great temple was so magnificent and architechtually brilliant - he spent so much time on it getting away from his wives' mothers.

☐

IN THE early days, when Taylors working were just starting to be used in military lodge a notice went round one lodge saying that in military masonry as in the army at the Ladies Festivals MM's had their ladies, FC's had their wives, whilst the EA's had their women. Roll on feminism .

☐

IT IS SAID that some masons get so pessimistic that when they smell the scent of flowers they look for a funeral.

Laughter at the Festive Board

□

A MASON came out of the lodge meeting and as he went into the street he slipped and fell, striking his head as he went down.

"Give him air" said the first man to reach him

"No, give the poor man some brandy," said a little old lady standing by.

"Call an ambulance" said another voice.

"Give him some brandy" continued the old lady.

"Get him to hospital" suggested another

"Give him some brandy" cried the old lady.

The fallen man looked up and said weakly:

"For God's sake won't anyone listen to the little old lady?"

□

A MASON invited his friend to a meeting where an FC was being raised. As happens sometimes they had trouble getting the car started and the traffic was bad. As a consequence they were very late for the initial part of the ritual. They came in after the brethren were finishing their teas and were all called back to hear the degree's long charge.

The visitor was soon dozing gently in the half light and the warmth of the room. The monotonous drone of the master giving the charge did not help. At one point he opened his eyes and said to his friend:

"That brother is word perfect but I wonder just how long he's been lecturing?"

"Oh, about four years."

"Thank the good lord. He should be finished soon."

□

"BRETHREN, THE meeting was particularly arduous for our Worshipful Master, who has had difficulties with his words today. As a consequence our

———————— **Laughter at the Festive Board** ————————

Worshipful Master would like to take wine with his prompters." At this, fifteen brothers stood up, their glasses raised to the Worshipful Master.

☐

MASONS have always been weary of telling jokes in pubs. They are aware that as soon as they do so some other mason will be reminded of a better one. Unfortunately, he will then step forward and prove that it is not.

☐

THE TWO children were playing a game when the little girl started to bellow at the little boy stamping around the drawing-room throwing cushions about.

Her mother rushed in to see what all the commotion was about.

"Joan, what do you think you are doing, making all that noise."

"Why, Mummy, Bobby and I are playing families."

"But why can't you be like Bobby he's not making any noise.?"

"Oh Mummy, you are silly. Of course Bobby isn't making any noise. He is Daddy coming home late from lodge and I am you welcoming him home."

☐

DURING THE lodge meeting a senior brother had a heart attack and the lodge was suspended whilst an ambulance was called.

As the brother was taken out on a stretcher one of the ambulance men said to the other: "Phew, I bet that was an initiation ceremony to remember."

☐

BROTHER BRENDAN Jones paid up all his dues and left his mother lodge. He obtained a certificate from the lodge secretary to say that he left without owing any dues.

He went to another lodge and asked to become a joining member. The first question that was asked was why he had left his mother lodge. He half smiled and said that it was for health reasons. Asked to expound a little more on this he confirmed that he had to leave because all the lodge had got sick and tired of him.

———————— **Laughter at the Festive Board** ————————

☐

MANY MASONS, these days seem to have Teflon minds, nothing seems to stick.

☐

THE HUMAN brain is the most wonderful thing given to man. It starts it's work in the womb long before the baby is born and continues until that baby becomes the master of his lodge and stops as soon as he starts to speak.

☐

IT IS said that the inactive mason is no more use than a corpse - but he takes up more room.

☐

BEWARE OF the brother who comes with an open mouth and a closed cheque book.

MURIEL, I REALLY DO WISH THAT YOU WERE MASTER OF MY LODGE - WE CHANGE OUR MASTER EVERY YEAR!

© COPYRIGHT GEOFFREY BRYAN 1995

THE AMERICAN mason was in London on business and was invited to visit a London lodge by his business acquaintance.

However, when he got to the lodge he was stopped by an officer who asked him for his lodge certificate which of course he had not brought with him.

"I must therefore put you to the test. What makes you a mason?"

"Well, I have been initiated into the craft up to Royal Arch, I am a 33° mason and am in Mark, Mariner and Templar."

"Sorry, but this isn't really the answer to my question? What makes you a mason?"

"Well, I contribute to all the charities and benevolence societies run by my lodge back in the states."

Again the brother shook his head and said:

"How about one last time. What makes you a mason?"

Scratching his head it suddenly dawned on him and he said with a big smile on his face:

"Of course, how silly of me it's this $500 reversible Masonic ring and the $1000 Masonic ball on my watch chain."

In despair he was allowed through the Tyler's door on the basis that they must make masons differently across the pond.

◻

DURING THE last war, London was almost raised to the ground. The number of unexploded bombs in and around the City made any journey hazardous.

A very obnoxious police superintendent was walking across a bombed plot when he was stopped by a very agitated army sergeant.

"Stop where you are, sir there is an unexploded bomb fifty feet away. It could go off at any second, we are waiting for the bomb disposal people to defuse it."

"I can't understand this at all. I've just passed a captain who is in my lodge, He must have seen me walking towards it, I wonder why he didn't say anything to warn me."

''Perhaps, he knows you, sir.''

◻

A MAN received a summons to attend court as a jury member on a certain day of the week. As he had some important business to do on that day he asked to be excused. He was summoned to attend before a law officer to see if his excuse for jury exemption was legitimate.

"Why do you wish to be excused from doing your duty as a juror?" asked the stern faced law officer.

""Well, sir, I am secretary of my lodge and we have a meeting on the afternoon of the day on which I am down for jury service."

"You seem to be giving yourself airs. Are you asking us to believe that you are totally indispensable in your lodge?"

"With respect, I know that I am not indispensable but I don't want my lodge brethren to find this out."

"Juror exempt," declared the law officer.

☐

AN INNER GUARD was asleep in bed with his dear wife when at two in the morning she thought she heard a noise outside of the back door.

She nudged her husband and whispered loudly into his ear:

"Ernest, I've just heard a noise outside, you did lock the back door, didn't you?"

Ernest sat bolt upright gently struck his wife several times on her forehead, put up his sign and staring at the mirror in his wife's dressing table opposite said in a monotone:

"Brother Junior Warden, the lodge is properly tyled." He then fell back to sleep on his pillow.

☐

"WORSHIPFUL BROTHER, as I will soon be your IPM, I must explain to you the true meaning of confidence. Confidence, especially Masonic confidence, is that quiet, absolutely assured feeling you will have just that split second before you fall flat onto your face."

☐

IT IS SAID by most Masonic grass widows that the average mason is forty around the chest, forty four around the waist, ninety six around the golf course and a damn nuisance around the house.

"ISN'T IT funny," said the treasurer "that some brothers can remember a joke but can't remember when their lodge subscriptions are due?"

☐

TO ERR is human but to forget totally usually means that you are in the chair.

☐

IF YOUR Masonry means much to you, live so it will mean as much to others.

☐

SOME MASONS use masonry like a wooden leg. There is neither life nor warmth in it; although it helps them to limp along it never becomes an actual part of them. And it has to be strapped on every morning.

☐

SOME MASONS grow under responsibility whilst others only swell.

☐

AT A LADIES FESTIVAL it was remarked to the head waiter that the coffee was not up to the standard required by the lodge. A note was returned by the head waiter to the president which just read "Please do not take the mickey out of our coffee - you may be sick and weak yourselves one day."

☐

THE GREATEST and noblest pleasure a man can have is to discover new truths and the next is to discard old prejudices.

☐

"MY BOY" a mason told his son who was about to be initiated, "you will learn that in lodge as in life lying about people annoys them very much, but sometimes telling the truth about them can annoy them a great deal more."

Laughter at the Festive Board

☐

WHAT A much better world we would have if we obeyed the Masonic rule that if we were at variance with another one or both should leave the lodge so that the lodge harmony would not be compromised.

☐

THE PRECEPTOR stood up with his sign
"Brethren, it's not for me now to whine.
But if you don't try
You'll never get by
And in office you never will shine."

☐

A MASON was leaving the Connaught Rooms at the end of his lodge's Festive Board. He turned into a side street and was confronted by a tramp who asked him for money. He felt sorry for the man and putting his hand into his pocket pulled out a £5 note which he gave him. The man thanked him and then offered him a drink from an old wine bottle. The mason smiled but declined the evil looking liquid. To his horror the tramp pulled out a screwdriver which was sharpened to a point and made him drink the liquid pointing the screwdriver at his benefactor's chest. When he had taken a large swig of the drink he shook his head and said almost falling over:

"That stuff is truly vile, I can't drink any more. You will have to use that thing on me."

"No mate," said the tramp "give me the bottle and this time you hold the screwdriver on me."

☐

SENIOR BRETHREN of a lodge in the Midlands are currently looking for an ex-member who left the lodge under a cloud and substituted non extinguishable candles for their third degree ritual.

☐

A MASON who was a great parrot breeder asked a brother to come and see the parrot he had taught.

Laughter at the Festive Board

When his friend saw the parrot in his cage sitting on his perch he noticed a pale blue ribbon tied to its left leg and a dark blue ribbon around its right leg. The end of each ribbon was hanging out of the cage. This intrigued him and he asked the parrot's owner what purpose these ribbons served.

"Well, Jim if you would care to pull the light blue ribbon the parrot will sing the lodge's opening hymn. If you pull the dark blue ribbon the parrot will sing the lodge's closing hymn."

"I'm very impressed. But what happens if I were to pull both ribbons?"

"Then I'd fall off the ruddy perch, you twerp," put in the parrot.

□

TWO LADIES were hoovering the lodge carpet after a meeting.

"Doris, why do they have a black and white squared carpet like this?"

"Well, Vi, I think that it's because it don't show the dirt like a white carpet would."

"But it shows the dirt in the white squares, don't it?"

"Violet, if these masons didn't have at least some sense of fairness me and you would be out of a job."

□

TWO TRAMPS were sitting down one evening to a light repast when one turned to the other and said:

"Were you ever in the Craft?"

"No, said the other "I never was. Why do you ask?"

"Well, I will show you something now that is very secret and was taught to me years ago when I was first made a mason." With that he ran a candle flame up and down the creases of the arm of his shirt.

"This my friend is what we masons call 'toasting the visitors'."

☐

A YOUNG MAN was being interviewed by several members of a Scottish lodge which he wished to join.

"Young man, if I was to ask you to name three of the most important freemasons in Scottish history could you do it?" asked the lodge secretary.

"Let me see now," the young man said, scratching his head, "well, obviously Robert Burns, then I suppose Sir Walter Scot and, oh, I'm sorry. what was your name again?"

☐

IN THE early thirties, an American film star was well known for his swashbuckling roles. He confirmed during an interview many years later that he had never had a fencing lesson in his life. He had gained his proficiency with a sword during his time as a Tyler of a lodge which had attracted lots of heavily armed eavesdroppers.

☐

TWO EXTREMELY old masons were talking in lodge prior to the arrival of the lodge officers.

"Bill, how long would you say that I have been in the craft?"

"Em," mused Bill, "let's see. Stand up and let me see your apron." He inspected his brother's apron, examined the gilt on the tassels and on the levels, "I'd say that you had been in the craft sixty two years seven months tomorrow."

"Bill you are amazing. You are exactly right to the very day. How could you possibly work that out?"

"Easy. You told me yesterday."

☐

A PRO GRAND Master was being chauffeured home after a Masonic engagement when he noticed a butcher's shop. He remembered that his wife had asked him to bring a leg of lamb home for the next day's meal. He asked the driver to stop and giving him a £10 note requested him to go and buy a large leg of lamb.

―――――― **Laughter at the Festive Board** ――――――

The chauffeur dutifully went into the shop and as he was being served the butcher glanced out of the window and said:

"Isn't that the Duke of ... shire, our PRO Grand Master?"

"I see that you are in the Craft," replied the chauffeur, "yes, it is he, and he's in a bit of a hurry and wants the leg of lamb for his dinner."

"Look, mate," said the butcher, "'you go and tell his nibs out there that if he gets rid of our old idiot of a lodge secretary, he can have the whole ruddy lamb."

BROTHER JOHN YOUR DISLIKE OF OUR CURRENT MASTER IS WELL KNOWN - NEVERTHELESS YOU WILL PUT UP THE PROPER SIGN - TWO FINGERS IS IN APPROPRIATE !!!

© COPYRIGHT GEOFFREY BRYAN 1995

JOE BLOGG's business was going down hill fast. You can imagine his joy when he spoke to a visitor at the Festive Board and found that they could do business together. The only thing was that the visitor had to have some specific details of the goods Joe could supply by 10 am next day. He was leaving his hotel then and it would be too late to give Joe a decision by the time he got back to his business.

The unfortunate thing was that Joe and his dear wife were in the middle of their monthly row. They were not speaking and they were going through the note stage of their row. When Joe got home his wife was out and as he was notorious for not hearing the alarm clock or even a telephone alarm call he left her a note pinned to her pillow asking (very nicely), to be called without fail at 7 next morning.

He had a very good sleep thinking of the great deal he was going to pull off. When he awoke at 10.15 am he found pinned to his pyjama jacket a note which read:

"THIS IS YOUR 7 O'CLOCK ALARM CALL - Mrs BLOGGS"

Laughter at the Festive Board

☐

TWO MASONS were talking over a drink at the Festive Board.

"It's my wife Valerie's birthday on Sunday and I haven't got her a present yet."

"Does she do a lot of gardening? If so I run a gardening shop outside of town. Come and see me Saturday and we can sort out something for her."

They met as agreed on Saturday and after a short while a dark green wheelbarrow was chosen as Valerie's birthday present.

"I bet your wife will be pleasantly surprised at this present."

"Oh, I know that she will be surprised. She's expecting a diamond ring."

☐

BILL AND BEN were lodge brothers and were discussing the merits of their respective wives.

"Ben, my wife really is as good as gold. I give her house keeping every Friday plus an allowance for her clothes and cosmetics. She rarely comes back for additions."

"Bill, you are so lucky. My wife is always asking for money. I estimate that she asks me for money every day. She wants £10 here and £20 there it really is a nightmare."

"What does she do with all this money, Ben?"

"I don't know. I never give her any."

☐

AT THE Ladies Night brother Fred couldn't find his wife and saw a large lady from the back wearing a dress that he vaguely remembered. As he had had more than a few drinks he went up to this apparition and pinched her bottom.

The apparition yelped and turned round and Fred saw to his horror that he had made a dreadful mistake.

Laughter at the Festive Board

"I - I - I am s-so terribly sorry. P-Please forgive me but l-l-l thought that you were my wife" he stammered.

"Your wife? You horrible, drunken little man. I feel so sorry for your wife married to a nasty, little creep like you."

"I - It's uncanny, w-why y-you even s-sound l-like her as well."

☐

ROBERT HAD been a guest of a brother at his lodge. He had had a long way to travel back home and after two hours driving he found that he was loosing concentration and decided to sleep it off so he pulled over to the side of the road to have a good sleep.

He was still very drowsy when he heard a tapping at his side window. It was a jogger who asked him for the correct time. Robert sleepily told him that it was 6.30 am and the man jogged off. Within fifteen minutes Robert was again woken by another jogger tapping on the window asking for the time. Robert was less than polite in sending him on his way.

So that he could sleep longer he took a piece of card from his brief case and in felt pen wrote in large letters "I DO NOT HAVE A WATCH" and placed the card in his window. He then took off his watch and placed it in his pocket.

He went off to sleep but again was awakened by a jogger tapping on the window. Bleary eyed he pulled down the window. The jogger smiled and said:

"It's 7 am mate." And jogged off.

☐

EA's do it with a 24 inch guage.

☐

FC's do it windingly.

☐

MM's do it darkly.

☐

THE LODGE secretary was a dour old Scot and looked over his glasses at the lodge idiot.

"Worshipful Brother Jock, I am applying for a new job. I would like your permission to be able to include your name and address on my Curriculum Vitaes someone who would give me a personal reference. You have known me in this lodge for four years now and I know that you would give me an honest reference."

Old Jock, nodded his head and said:

"Laddie, 'tis true I've known y' for many years, aye, I could gi' you a reference, aye and it would be honest, never fear. But I feel, in m' heart o' hearts, that y'd do much, much better without it."

☐

JOHN TOOK SAM to his lodge meeting on Saturday as his guest. Sam had an enjoyable meeting and suggested that he responded to John's kindness by taking him to his golf club on Sunday for a round of golf finished off with a fine meal at the nineteenth hole. Although John did not know one end of a golf iron or wood from the other he agreed to go with Sam as long as he was shown what to do and not be made to look a complete idiot.

Sam showed John how to hold the club, where to put the tee in the ground and how to place the golf ball on it. Sam went through the golf swing several times and told John not to take his eye off the ball and aim for the flag some three hundred yards away.

John did as he was bid and his swing sent the ball straight and true. It landed some eighteen inches from the hole.

"Now what do I do?" asked John.

"Well, you have now got a short putt to get the ball into the hole."

"Thank you, very much Sam," sneered John, "it would have saved me much time and trouble if you had told me that in the first place."

Laughter at the Festive Board

☐

THE LODGE Tyler had a terrible bronchitis attack at the Festive Board and was unable to recite the Tyler's Toast. The master was very concerned about his health and arranged for him to see his own consultant.

The consultant examined the Tyler and said:

"Look old chap, your lungs are really congested. Cut out the cigarettes and take this linctus every other day do you understand?"

The Tyler looked blankly at the consultant who said:

"You are a prime candidate for emphysema and must not smoke any more, do you understand?" The Tyler nodded. "Good, and you must take this linctus on alternate days. That is take it today, skip tomorrow, take it the next day, skip the day after. Do you understand. If you don't keep to these instructions you won't last long" The Tyler nodded and thanked him for his time and took the bottle of linctus with him.

Some weeks later the Tyler's wife went to see the consultant and he asked how her husband was.

"He's dead. I buried him a fortnight ago."

The consultant was visibly shocked and asked:

"I did tell him that he would die if he didn't keep to my specific instructions?"

"He carried out your instructions to the letter. That's what killed him - all that ruddy skipping."

☐

TWO MEN went into their local pub and met a third who was known to one of them.

"This is my friend Tim, who is a bit of a wag."

The other smiled and offered his hand to Tim who squeezed it in a finger crushing hand shake.

─────────── Laughter at the Festive Board ───────────

"What the hell is this?" asked the one whose hand was caught in the vice.

"Oh, it's only an FA's token," laughed Tim as he squeezed the hand harder.

"Well, if you would just like to release me for a moment, I will let you feel an MM's maul."

☐

THREE MASONS were in France at the time when Napoleon Bonapart had taken imperial power. They had acted suspiciously and were taken into custody as spies against the French Empire.

The three, two Englishmen and an Irishman, protested their innocence but they were found guilty and condemned to death.

They all made entreaties to the court but they stood condemned. They even wrote to the Emperor as fellow masons but received his message that as the Grand Master of the Antients, the Prince Regent, had been so rude about him and the French people they must die. He hoped that they would die with courage as was expected of masons.

The first Englishman was hoodwinked and put on the plank of the guillotine and the blade came down but stopped within two inches of his neck. This happened twice more and by French custom he was released.

The guillotine was tested and found to be all right and the second Englishman was put on the plank. Exactly the same thing happened to him as to his friend and after three attempts he, too, was released.

Again the death mechanism was checked over and tested and the Irishman was brought out. They were about to tie his blindfold and he said:

"People of France I will show you how an Irishman will die. No hoodwink for me and I will face the blade."

The crowd cheered and the Irishman was put on the plank facing the blade above him. The executioner, Sanson, released the blade and it came whistling down but it too stopped a few inches from the exposed neck.

The Irishman, from his position under the blade, looked to the left and to the right of the frame and said:

"There's your trouble, lads, that screw on the right is too loose. When someone is put on the plank the screw stops the blade from falling properly. Tighten up the screw and the blade will slice through anything."

☐

LODGE TREASURERS never die they only lose their reconciliations.

☐

THE NEW STEWARD was going around with the wine at the Festive Board. He went up to one brother and said:

"Would you like wine, brother John?"

"Yes please, I would like rosé if you have it."

"Certainly, sir, red or white?"

☐

THE OLD mason lay dying and as his wife was tidying the bed asked him if she could do anything to make him more comfortable.

"If it's not too much trouble I would like a small cigar, it can't hurt me now, can it?"

She smiled and gave him a cigar and lit it for him.

"Also if it's not too much trouble could you hand me my small Masonic book?"

She handed him his book.

"Thank you, my darling," he smiled, "could I trouble you once more. May I have a small glass of whisky?"

"I am sorry, love, but I can let you have the whisky. It's needed for the party after the funeral."

☐

JUNIOR WARDENS do it at High Time

IF MASTERS are real EastEnders does that make *SENIOR WARDENs* Westenders?

□

A MASON asked a friend from work if he wanted to attend his next meeting. The meeting went well but at the Festive Board the caterers were replaced at the last minute and the portions given to the brethren were less than adequate.

The friend said very little when the soup was served. It was very thin and tasteless and only a small ladle was put into each brothers' soup bowl.

The main course was roast lamb but the slices were so thin they were transparent.

"Excuse me, miss," said the visitor to the waitress, "did you cut this meat?"

"As a matter of fact I did. Why got any complaints?" she replied gruffly.

"Certainly not, my dear. But it's only fair if you cut you must let me deal."

□

SENIOR DEACONS only carry tales.

□

TWO MASONS were talking in lodge and were mulling over the delights of the world when one said to the other:

"Brother John, if you could wish for anything what would be the best thing you would wish for?"

"I would wish for an ocean going yacht. What would you wish for, brother Philip?"

"I would wish for Joanna Lumley."

"Oh come off it, Philip; you said the best thing not the very best thing."

Laughter at the Festive Board

☐

IT WAS the most important meeting of the decade. The lodge banner was to be dedicated. The lodge had even brought in a famous industrialist who was a well known speaker on Masonic subjects.

Before the Festive Board a young mason went up to the industrialist while he was washing his hands and said;

"Sir Robert, I am new to the world of industry but if during the evening you could come up to me whilst I am with my friends and ask me how I'm getting along it would boost my credit with everyone to know someone as truly famous as you. My name's Raymond by the way."

Sir Robert smiled and said that he would be delighted to help the young man if he could.

Ater the meal and the subsequent toast and speeches, in which Sir Robert was excellent, several groups formed and brothers were talking and laughing. Sir Robert went up to one group and patting the young man on the back said:

"Raymond, I'm so glad to see you here. How are you keeping?"

Raymond turned from his group and said:

"Not now Bob, can't you see I'm talking business."

☐

A MASON arrived home from a meeting and found his wife asleep in bed. The next day he couldn't hear his wife at all. He let this go on for another day and decided to see his doctor. However, before he made the appointment his wife came back from the doctor's surgery with some throat spray. Apparently she had laryngitis, for all these days he thought that he had gone completely deaf.

☐

OLD ALMONERS never die they just have trouble opening their purses.

☐

BEFORE THE war freemasons in Germany were having a hard time. Many were sent to concentration camps for "rehabilitation". Initially in the early 1930's brethren were told that they could earn good wages at these camps and two masons who were blacklisted from employment in normal jobs decided to go to one of these camps.

"Ludwig," said Karl "let me try the camp first. If it's as good as the government says at these camps I will confirm it. If it's not I'll let you know so that you won't volunteer."

"That's a good idea, but we should have some sort of code as I am sure the authorities will censor all letters from the camps. I know if your letter is written in blue or black ink then everything you write is true. But if it is written in green ink everything in it is false."

This was agreed and over the weeks Ludwig waited for his friend's letter from the camp. Within three weeks he received Karl's first letter-written in blue ink.

The letter was buzing with a glowing report of the good food and accommodation at the camp and the people in charge of the camp although wearing SS uniforms were some of the friendliest he had met. The only unfortunate note in the letter was the PS which said "Only disappointment here is that GREEN INK is unavailable."

☐

OLD INNER GUARDS never die they just forget to point their poniards.

☐

AN AMERICAN MASON was the guest of an English mason at a meeting. Before they went to the Festive Board they went to the bar for a drink. The American bought his friend a lager and then said to the barman:

"Son, I'm from the US of A, and I want a very, very Dry Martini. Do you think you can do me one. Its got to be fifteen parts London Dry Gin to one part extra dry vermouth."

"Certainly sir" replied the barman with a big smile, "would you like me to twist the rind of a lemon over the Martini?"

"Son, son," agonised the American brother "if I'd have wanted a lemonade I would have asked you for one."

Laughter at the Festive Board

☐

OLD LODGE ORGANISTS never die they just exchange their organs for harps.

☐

AN EMINENT mason who was also a brilliant botanist brought some lovely blue grey mushrooms home and gave instructions to his wife on how to cook them.

"These are unusual mushrooms, darling, where did you get them?"

"From the small wood on the way home. They really are fabulous aren't they darling?"

His wife loved mushrooms so she cooked them and as they were so moorish she ate the lot. Next morning her husband said to her at breakfast:

"How did you sleep, darling?"

"Marvellously." she replied.

"No headaches, nausea or swollen tongue?"

"Silly old you. Why do you ask?"

He threw up his arms into the air and jumped up and shouted:

"Fantastic, really fantastic. I've only discovered a mutated funghi that's no longer poisonous to women. I wonder if it would be OK for masons at the Festive Board?"

☐

STEWARDS do it at the Festive Board.

☐

MASONS do it regularly.

☐

THE LODGE TREASURER was putting transactions through the lodge

Laughter at the Festive Board

accounts one afternoon when he got a telephone call from the Inspector of Taxes.

"We are currently looking at the tax return of a Mr John Smith, who has told us that he is a member of your lodge. He has put down that in the last tax year he gave £2,000 to the lodge charities and is claiming tax relief on that amount. Would you confirm that you have received this amount from him?"

"I can confirm that John Smith is a member of the lodge but he would have paid any moneys to our Charity Steward. It may be in the account or it may still be with the Charity Steward. But, let me assure you that whether we have Mr Smith's money or not, we will have his money in our accounts by tomorrow at the latest."

☐

THE TWO masons sat at the bar after the meeting.

"I think meeting on a Saturday is the only draw back to this lodge, because we miss all the great sporting events that they show on Television on Saturday afternoons."

"Don't talk to me about TV. In my job as a TV licence investigator I have to find out more about people's TV's and whether they have bought their annual licences."

"Take for example what happened yesterday. I called at a house in my detector van just as the lady of the house was coming out. When I asked her if she had a TV because I couldn't find from my computer printout that she had a licence. She told me that they had bought the set on Wednesday and bought the licence yesterday. I asked if she would show me the licence but she said that she was in a hurry. She said that her husband would be back around 2 pm and he would show me the licence which she had put under the clock on the dining room mantelpiece."

"I returned at 3 pm and her husband came to the door."

"Excuse me, would you please show me your current TV licence?" I asked him.

"Sorry, mate" he replied, "I'm sure that we have one but I don't know where it is at this time"

"I think, sir, that the current licence is under the clock on the dining room mantelpiece."

Laughter at the Festive Board

He went away and came back a few moments later carrying the licence.

"I know that the TV licensing bureau are always telling the public just how powerful the detector van is and how it can tell what TV channel you are watching. But, to be able to tell you exactly where your licence is in the house is really remarkable."

☐

OLD LODGE CHAPLAINS never die they just close the VSL

☐

LODGE STEWARDS do it at the Festive Board.

☐

THEN THERE was the rather naive brother who was asked to be a steward at the Festive Board at the start of his lodge office. He requested a snug 16 inch collar size.

☐

CANDIDATES do it with much caution.

☐

AN ENGLISH MASON went to New York as the guest of honour at the bicentennial of a Scottish Rite's lodge. He had time to kill and he decided to walk around Central Park. After ten minutes in the park a jogger knocked him and he fell over. Instinctively checking his pocket discovered his wallet gone. He ran after the jogger and grabbing him from behind shouted: "Wallet. Wallet! You creep."

The jogger hurriedly gave him the wallet and with a crimson face rushed off.

When the mason returned to his hotel room he went to close his regalia case which was on the bed and there to his horror discovered his own wallet on top of his apron and gloves.

☐

TWO LIONS escaped from the London Zoo and went their separate ways.

After four months they met up with each other. One had grown excessively fat whilst the other appeared not to have eaten for some time.

"I've never seen a lion looking so well fed. Where have you been eating?" asked the malnourished one.

"It's dead easy. I've been sleeping around Freemason's Hall in London and looking out for Grand Lodge Officers - they are the ones with the large black bags. I've been eating one Grand Lodge Officer a day. So far no one has noticed they're missing."

☐

TWO MASONS who had been lodge brothers for forty years decided to spend fifty pence each on a lottery ticket. They used their ages and lodge number and used them on the lottery ticket. Between them they won eight million pounds.

They decided to go to London and whilst looking around saw two beautiful Jaguar cars in a showroom. They both had a price tag of sixty thousand pounds each and Joe asked Josh if he wanted a car. Josh agreed that he did and Joe went in and after a phone call to his bank to confirm that he held the funds bought the two cars which would be delivered to them in the following week.

They continued to look around the shops and spent some hours looking at the Masonic Peace Memorial in Great Queen Street. Around four pm they became hungry and walking into Kingsway they saw a man selling hamburgers from a van.

"Fancy a hamburger, Joe?" asked Josh.

"Yes, please, with plenty of onions. Here you are here's a fiver."

"No, no, Joe, I'll get these. You paid for the cars."

☐

TWO LITTLE BOYS were talking and one said to the other:

"My daddy knows your daddy because they both go to the same lodge. My daddy's told my mummy that your daddy helps animals that are poorly."

"Why do you say my daddy helps poorly animals. That's not right. My daddy hates cats and dogs and things. How does your daddy know?"

Laughter at the Festive Board

"Well I heard my daddy tell my mummy that he was in the betting shop and said that your daddy put his shirt on a bleeding horse that was scratched."

☐

TWO CONSULTANTS who were in the same lodge came out of a meeting after the nine o'clock toast when they saw walking on the opposite side of the road an extremely good looking young lady.

"Jeremy, look at the boobs on that young lady."

"I'm not interested, old boy. I'm an ear, nose and throat man myself."

☐

A TEENAGER was given a project to do for his school. It was on 'Freemasonry'. He had no knowledge on the subject and asked his father who was a mason.

"Well, son, I can think of no better book on the subject as Coil's three volume "History of Freemasonry". You may borrow my set as long as you don't damage it."

The books were given over to the teenager but although he spent many hours going through the books his project did not get him a good mark because he only wrote one paragraph which said:

"Coil's "History of Freemasonry" in three volumes has told me more about Freemasonry than I really wanted to know."

☐

THE PRECEPTOR was talking to the Master and said:

"Brother Graham is really a pain in the bottom. He is the most negative brother at the Lodge of Instruction and queries every decision I make. He talks loudly through all the rituals we practice. He is gathering a small nucleus of disenchanted brothers around him. I wish we could get rid of him. The only thing is that he is the only brother at the LOI who has a hundred per cent attendance

☐

JUNIOR DEACONS do it by turning over the tracing boards.

─────── **Laughter at the Festive Board** ───────

◻

IN SOME American lodges in the cowboy states the cable tow is a normal full sized lariat. The only trouble is that the officer holding it has on occasions been carried away and rather than just putting it on insists on lassoing the candidate from a running start. This isn't too bad but sometimes the officer forgets himself completely, pulls the candidate over and ties him up ready for branding.

◻

A DISTINGUISHED mason was hired by the lodge to give a talk on various Egyptian rites. Unfortunately, one of the brethren had had a very good liquid lunch and had reinforced that lunch with an evening session. He did a good deal of laughing at the speaker and interrupted him on a number of occasions before two lodge officers got him out of his seat to take him from the hall.

"Why, young man," said the speaker, "we could well be a double act. I could sing 'Moon River'."

"What could I do?" enquired the drunken brother.

"Jump into it."

AN ELDERLY mason, who would now be called folicularly challenged, or almost bald, went to get his hair cut. As he sat in the chair the barber came up to him and said:

"Has sir a particular style, that sir requires?"

"Sir, I am over eighty and my hair is only a little younger. I have too few resources left on my head to have a hair style. Just get on and when you find hair - cut it ."

☐

OLD SENIOR WARDENS never die they just can't find their level.

☐

AN OLD LODGE acquired a new master
But his working got faster and faster
His officers couldn't refrain
From saying again and again
"Hold, Stop, Quit-you are a disaster"

☐

FRED WAS a self-made man and joined a local lodge. He felt extremely inferior as several members were titled and he wanted them to look up to him and not despise him as noveau riche.

He decided to pay a genealogist £10,000 to trace his antecedents. Unfortunately, when the genealogist came up with the details of his family tree it cost him another £20,000 to hush it all up.

☐

TWO REGALIA makers, Maurice and Sidney, were in a pub bemoaning the fact that there were so few candidates going through lodges, and fewer masons meant fewer aprons were being sold. They calculated that unless they sold the 20,000 aprons they had in stock at £5 each they would be bankrupt before the week was out. As they talked a big American in a wide Stetson came over to them and introduced himself to them.

"Hi, my name is Hiram Bigalow, and I am buying Masonic regalia for my Masonic Craft Emporium in Dallas, Texas. I understand that you are regalia makers and might be able to help me. I am particularly interested in buying English Master Mason blue aprons. I'm looking to buy 20, 000 if the price is right."

The two looked at each other and coughed and spluttered.

"We just be able to help you. But we could not sell them for less than £7 each."

"Well that would be around $200,000 in real money. It's a little more than I was expecting to pay but the dollar is going down. Before I could give you a final answer I would have to get the OK from my financial director. I will be back home tomorrow. I'm sure he will agree to your price. Give me your telephone number and if you don't get a telephone call from me by 6 pm, your time, tomorrow the deals on."

The two went home so happy but they neither could sleep and when they went into the office next day they were on tenter hooks wondering whether they would receive the dreaded telephone call.

It was now 5.58 pm and no call had been received from Hiram Bigalow. Then just as the clock started to chime 6 the phone rang. They both went pale and Maurice picked up the phone. Within a few seconds his eyes were wide open and a big grin came over his face. He held the phone towards the other and said:

"'Sidney, Sidney, great news - your mother's dead."

☐

A **MASON** should cultivate brevity
But with just that degree of levity
For nothing is worse
Than being too terse
By testing the listener's longevity.

☐

OLD JUNIOR WARDENS never die they just go out of plumb.

☐

A VICAR who was chaplain at his lodge was normally a very tidy person, but when it came to his Masonic regalia he was a real slob. If he didn't leave his regalia case in the kitchen he left it in the bedroom doorway. His white gloves which were to be washed were stuffed unceremoniously in his chest of drawers. His wife was in desperation and said:

"Archibald, if you don't tidy up your Masonic bits and pieces I will throw them out. I am not joking."

"My dear heart, please remember the sayings of Jesus that you should forgive a man his sins not seven times but seventy times seven."

"Very well, but do in four hundred and ninety one times more and out they go "

☐

I HAVE HEARD that there are lodges in the USA with over five thousand members. Apparently the lodges have to have their meetings in covered football stadia. The Tyler has to use an armoured car to patrol the outside area. The workings are all on closed circuit Television and all the officers have to use microphones.

In comparison our lodge is so small that when you sit near the inner guard and whisper something the master stops the meeting and requests that you stop prompting him.

☐

WORSHIPFUL BROTHER Bob Simpson had been a devoted member of his lodge for over forty years. He had been a founder member of four other lodges. It had been a hectic Masonic career and although he had loved every minute he was near to total exhaustion.

His doctor recommended that he take a complete break from his Masonic duties and although he fought against it, he had to admit that he didn't fight that hard.

His devoted wife had been both a firm support and a sounding board for his ideas and when he confirmed that he was going to have a rest she was delighted.

"Bob, that's the best news I've heard today," she agreed.

"Let's go abroad and have the honeymoon we never had all those years ago when we first got married. Where would you like to go; Bermuda, Jamaica ?"

"'Well, Bob, if it's all right by you I think that a week at Lourdes wouldn't go amiss."

☐

OLD REGALIA MAKERS never die that just can't thread their needles.

☐

THE BANK MANAGER had been in the craft for over forty years and had obtained the Past Master's aprons and lodge medals of five lodges and one chapter. He had taken London Grand Rank and was a noted authority on the Emulation Ritual.

One day a young man came to a see him for a position in the bank. The friendly old manager quickly put the man at his ease and offered him a cup of coffee while they discussed the man's possible career with the bank.

The manager's vast experience with dealing with people at all levels both in and out of the craft made him an ideal person to find the real motivation behind a the normal smoke screen put up by the inteviewee.

"Young man, why do you wish to join the Westlands Bank?" He asked.

"Well you have read my CV and you will see that I like people and have good numeric skills,"

"How would you, for instance, deal with a customer who came in and told you that he wanted to see me and that although he didn't have an appointment he was a Freemason and thought that he should be allowed to jump the queue?"

"Oh, that's very easy. Anyone whose a freemason is always corrupt, is cunning and secretive and will do anything to get on." He said with a big smirk on his face as he sat back into his chair, "I wouldn't have a bar of anyone daring to admit that they were freemasons."

"Well, my boy, you certainly forthright in your opinions. I'm glad you can speak to me openly of your views about freemasons. I am afraid, however, that we have no openings for chaps with your obvious talents.

"I would suggest that you go and join the Samaritans where your reserve and tack will stand you in good stead with anyone contemplating suicide."

☐

"I REGRET that Worshipful Brother John, the Master of Ceremony, will not be attending lodge for the next few months," intoned the secretary at the regular meeting, "apparently he was showing the brother junior deacon a particularly forceful golf swing with the deacon's wand and has managed to break his leg in two places."

"I'll bet he won't be going to those places again," whispered the lodge chaplain.

☐

"DO YOU know why English is called the Mother Tongue?" A mason asked his young son.

"It's because, at home, father is never allowed to open his mouth."

☐

CANDIDATES are hoodwinked into doing it.

☐

A VERY SENIOR mason was having a quiet drink with a friend at a hostelry in Great Queen Street when a complete stranger carrying a masonic regalia case came up to him and said:

"Whato, 'Arry, how's it going then? Still conning the masses?"

"Sir, I know neither your name nor your face but your manners are very familiar."

☐

A SPEAKER at the Festive Board went on for over fifty minutes. At first the brethren enjoyed his witticism but as the speech went on and on voices were being raised and when eventually the speaker closed he said:

"Brethren, please forgive me for speaking so long. My watch has stopped and I forgot the time."

A brother stood up and said:

"You may not have had a watch to look at but can't you see that calendar on the wall opposite?"

THE GAMBLING TYLER

The candidate sat in a bit of a state
The Tyler was absent. - he really was late
The master was sorry for keeping it dark
But without the old Tyler they were short of the mark

At last the old boy with his apron askew
Rushed in through the door and sat down on a pew
"My boy you will learn of our own secret lore
Of our own hidden craft that base cowans explore

But remember young man as you go through that door
That out here sits a man with a sword in his paw
A man who cannot look brave in his apron and collar
Without putting on a bet with his last half a dollar."

☐

AT THE Festive Board one of the speakers was going on and on but no amount of coughing by brethren could stop him. He was finally prompted to sit down when the oldest member, who was almost ninety two said in a very loud stage whisper:

"Doesn't that youngster realise that there are some of us here who haven't long to go?"

☐

"DAD," the lewis said to his father, "how can you tell if a man and woman are married if neither of them wear wedding rings."

"That's easy son. If the man washes the lady's car then they are just in love If she washes the car then they are married."

☐

TWO ESSEX masons, who were cricket fanatics, were watching Essex play at the county ground at Chelmsford. One of them put his hand into his pocket and found to his horror that he had left his wallet back home in Wickford. He excused himself and took his car back home.

―――――――――――― **Laughter at the Festive Board** ――――――――――――

When he returned he was looking extremely upset as was his companion.

"Bill, I've got some terrible news for you. Your Rolls Royce in the car park has been hit by someone and he has taken the side off. It's going to cost an arm and a leg to get that repaired."

Bill looked up, very pale and said "I've got some bad news for you too. Gooch is out."

☐

A MASON returning from a meeting and having dined well at the Festive Board got the taxi driver to drop him outside his house. He paid off the taxi and instead of walking the front path to his front door walked across his lawn and walked straight into a large cherry tree the sole occupant of his lawn.

He rubbed his head and walked to his right but in his dazed and somewhat inebriated state turned and struck the tree again. He turned to his left and again tried to walk away from the tree but zig zagged back and struck the tree for a third time this time the force knocked him to the ground.

With a great effort he stood up and using the tree as a support looked up to the moon in the night sky and said:

"Look, if you get me out of this ruddy enchanted forest I promise to join a dry lodge as soon as I can."

☐

SANDY had been a mason for forty years but his lodge secretary, who hadn't seen him in lodge for six months, was surprised to have a letter from him stating that he wished to leave the lodge. The secretary telephoned him to ask the reason why he wished to leave.

"Well, Brother Secretary, I have lost one of my white cotton gloves and I have no wish to go to the great expense of buying another pair when I only require one. I consider that I have two ways of staying in lodge. One is to keep my ungloved hand in my pocket during the rituals. The other option is for me to have one hand cut off but I think just leaving the lodge will save me from much pain and even more expense."

☐

MANY YEARS AGO a middle-aged mason decided to go to the market place to buy some lettuces. As he was looking at one stall he felt very uneasy and turning round came face to face with Death. The look on the face of Death threw the mason into a panic and he rushed home as fast as he could.

He explained to his wife had happened and told her that he must hide from Death.

"My husband, where can you go where Death will not think of looking for you?" she asked.

"I know. I will go to my lodge room which is twenty miles away. I never go there during the week and so Death will have no reason to look for me there."

With that he rushed off leaving his distraught wife alone.

His wife was so unhappy that Death had so frightened her husband that she went to the market to confront him.

When she got to the market Death was sitting on a kerb stone looking very puzzled.

"Why did you frighten my husband so this morning?" she enquired of him.

"My dear lady when I came across your husband in the market it took me completely by surprise for, you see, I have an appointment with him this afternoon at his lodge room which is many miles from here. I couldn't see how he was going to make it there in time."

☐

TWO LADIES at the Ladies Festival were talking about their respective husbands.

"My George will be master next year and he will have a really fantastic year. He's only forty five and will see many years in the lodge," said one matron, "I think that he is like gold dust to me.".

"Well, dear, my Derek is in the chair now and it happens to be his fifty ninth birthday today. He is not really like gold dust more like a large denomination note. When he gets to sixty I'm going to exchange him for three twenties."

☐

HOW MANY MASONs does it take to tile a lodge? It depends on how thin you slice them.

Laughter at the Festive Board

☐

A MASON had to go to hospital for a check up. He was introduced to the consultant, who happened to be on the square, and they got chatting.

"How long have you be in the craft?" asked the consultant.

"Oh, about twenty years now," the mason replied.

"I find it a bit difficult to be able to attend meetings, because of the hours I have to work in the hospital. But I have managed to get all the masons in my lodge onto my private books so before every meeting I have all the members who wish to do so consult me in the Tyler's ante room. The brethren get a consultant's undivided attention and I get enough in the way of consultation fees to provide me with enough for my lodge dues the charities and two visits to the Caribbean on the QE2 a year."

☐

A MASON got on a bus after his lodge meeting and festive board. He paid his fare to the conductor who happened to notice his regalia case.

"A mason, I see" said the conductor, "you use this bus quite regularly don't you?"

"Yes I do, I go to my lodge of instruction every Thursday evening and to my main lodge four times a year on a Friday afternoon and pick up this bus in the evening."

"You were on this bus yesterday, weren't you?" suggested the conductor,"and had had a real skinful by the time you'd got on."

"Why do you say that. I rarely have more than two drinks after the lodge of instruction."

"Last night must have been special because when you were about to get off yesterday night you insisted that a lady take your seat."

"What's wrong with that. I might have been merry but I still consider myself a gentleman."

"There's nothing wrong with that, but for two small facts. First, when you insisted that the lady took your seat there were only you two passengers on the bus. And second, she was also getting off at the same stop as you."

―――――――――――― **Laughter at the Festive Board** ――――――――――――

☐

A MISSOURI farmer was called upon by a cattle foodstuffs salesman. During their talk the salesman noticed a large portrait of Pope Pius Xll in skull cap and white cassock. The salesman thought this was odd and said to the farmer:

"Mr Jackson, sir, I am truly surprised at you having a portrait of the pope on your walls, I always understood that you were a Methodist."

"What are you talking about, sir? I have been a Mehodist for over sixty years now and in no way would I have a picture of that papist pope on my walls."

"Well, sir I can assure you that that there picture is of the current pope."

"God blame me, it was one of you salesmen fellers who sold me that there picture. The onery critter told me that it was President Harry S Truman in his Masonic regalia."

☐

THE LODGE TREASURER was a serving police inspector and whilst he was at the Festive Board he overheard a visitor, the guest of the lodge secretary, talking to another brother. He was not eavesdropping but couldn't help hearing snippets of his conversation. He heard "terrible case, spine broken and appendix missing...."

He was intrigued at this and interrupted the visitor and said:

"Excuse me for butting in but I couldn't help hearing your conversation. Do you happen to be a Home Office Pathologist or forensic scientist?"

"Oh, my goodness, no," smiled the visitor, "I'm a book-binder and repairer."

☐

THE CHEF STEWARD responsible for the food preparation at the Festive Board had received a number of complaints from the brethren about the food. A brother suggested getting another chef and told him of a Nepalese chef who prepared food for a neighbouring lodge and produced a masterpiece, called in the native dialect 'Poi'.

The chief steward went to see the Chef and asked if he would prepare the 'Poi' for the lodge. The Chef, in his broken English, haggled over the price per head and said that under no circumstances would he divulge the recipe, which were passed to him by his headman of his village. The steward agreed that the 'Poi' secret would remain with the chef.

The Chef nodded his acceptance of the terms under which he would prepare his delicacy and then asked:

"What kind Poi you want? I make two kinds: Sheferd's Poi or Steak Kidley Poi"

☐

THE LODGE SECRETARY stood up at the third time of asking and said to the Worshipful Master:

"Wor. Master, I have a request from W. Bro Smith, the landlord of the public house downstairs and of this lodge room. He humbly requests that from now on you and future occupiers of the Seat Of Solomon 'do' at least four 'Thirds' in each Masonic year."

"That's a strange request, W. Bro. Secretary. What interest does our brother landlord have in this lodge 'doing' so many third degrees?"

"Very simple Worshipful Master, you see less candles used mean less soot from him to remove annually from the ceiling."

☐

TWO MEN sat opposite each other on a train. It became very hot and stuffy and one man said to the other:

"Ex - ex- excuse me, b - b- but w - w- would y-y - you mind if I - I - op -o opened the w- w-window'."

"Certainly not" replied the other and the man opened the window. As the man sat down the other said:

"Going far'

"O-O-Oh y-y-yes, t-to L-L-London. I - I - I've g-g-got an in-in-interview at the B-b-b, B-b- b C-c-c as an an- an -announcer."

"Do you think you will get it?" asked the incredulous man.

"Sh-sh-shouldn't the-the-think s-s-so. You see I'm n-n-not a r-r-ruddy mason."

Laughter at the Festive Board

☐

STANLEY had saved all his life and when he retired he went on a world cruise. As he had been in the Craft for over forty years he took his regalia case with him on the cruise just in case he was invited to a lodge meeting whilst he was on his trip.

Unfortuneately, whilst he was in the Pacific an accident in the cruise ship's boiler room cast everyone adrift on the high seas. The only thing Stanley could save was his regalia case.

After he was alone in the water for two hours high seas drove him onto a Pacific Island. Three men, all speaking English, pulled him from the surf. They gave him food and drink and seeing his regalia case told him that they had founded a lodge on the island and that he was invited to attend the next meeting as their guest.

Stanley, enjoyed himself so much that he went up to the current master and said:

"Worshipful Master, I would be honoured if you would allow me to join your lodge. I am experienced in Emulation and would be proud to join in the day to day running of the lodge,"

"Brother Stanley, as much as we all welcome you to our Island and to our lodge we all regret that we cannot accept you as a joining member. You see we are all shipwrecked ten years ago whilst on a beano from a non alcoholic Police Lodge in Aberystwyth and it is so unfortunate that you are not a non alcoholic Welsh policeman.."

☐

WILLIAM was transfered by his firm to a small town in Gloucester and he leased a small cottage in a very picturesque village. As a man who enjoyed his masonry he asked around about the lodges nearby and was happy to find that there were two lodges in his village. Both lodges were held in large rooms over the village's two public houses. He decided to look at both lodges to see which would suit him.

He asked the landlord of each pub which lodge was best but, of course, he received good reports from both. In desparation he spoke to the senior police office in the village whose judgment he trusted.

"Well, my boy," smiled the policeman, "if you wish to be a joining member of either lodge I think that you will be sorely disappointed. Because, whichever lodge you chose, I can assure you that you will soon wish that you have chosen the other."

☐ ☐ ☐